"*How to Find Out Anything* is an indispensable guide to the information age. It's written with great clarity and wit, and crammed with useful tips and resources, as well as sage advice on how to organize and plan your research. My only complaint is that it didn't come out a long time ago. It would have saved me a lot of time and frustration."

—**John Strausbaugh, author and journalist**

"I use Don's tips every day at my proofreading job and for my own writing research. I'd love to sing his praises on the record. I do so daily, as it is."

—**Leigh Angel, proofreader**

"I remember one thing in particular that Don said—something to the effect of no matter how obscure an interest or passion may be, if there are two people in the world who share it, they will find each other and they will form an association! I thought that was hysterical and it's true! Don taught me how to Google in a whole new way!"

—**Jen Fernicola Ronay, attorney**

How to Find Out Anything

From Extreme Google Searches to Scouring
Government Documents, a Guide to Uncovering
Anything About Everyone and Everything

DON MACLEOD

PRENTICE HALL PRESS

PRENTICE HALL PRESS
Published by the Penguin Group
Penguin Group (USA) Inc.
375 Hudson Street, New York, New York 10014, USA
Penguin Group (Canada), 90 Eglinton Avenue East, Suite 700, Toronto, Ontario M4P 2Y3, Canada
(a division of Pearson Penguin Canada Inc.) • Penguin Books Ltd., 80 Strand, London WC2R 0RL,
England • Penguin Group Ireland, 25 St. Stephen's Green, Dublin 2, Ireland (a division of Penguin
Books Ltd.) • Penguin Group (Australia), 250 Camberwell Road, Camberwell, Victoria 3124, Australia
(a division of Pearson Australia Group Pty. Ltd.) • Penguin Books India Pvt. Ltd., 11 Community
Centre, Panchsheel Park, New Delhi—110 017, India • Penguin Group (NZ), 67 Apollo Drive,
Rosedale, Auckland 0632, New Zealand (a division of Pearson New Zealand Ltd.) • Penguin Books
(South Africa) (Pty.) Ltd., 24 Sturdee Avenue, Rosebank, Johannesburg 2196, South Africa

Penguin Books Ltd., Registered Offices: 80 Strand, London WC2R 0RL, England

While the author has made every effort to provide accurate telephone numbers, Internet addresses,
and other contact information at the time of publication, neither the publisher nor the author assumes
any responsibility for errors or for changes that occur after publication. Further, the publisher does
not have any control over and does not assume any responsibility for author or third-party
websites or their content.

First edition: August 2012

Library of Congress Cataloging-in-Publication Data

MacLeod, Don, 1955–
How to find out anything : from extreme Google searches to scouring government documents, a guide to
uncovering anything about everyone and everything / Don MacLeod.—First edition.
pages   cm
Includes index.
ISBN 978-0-7352-0467-6 (pbk.)
1. Research—Methodology.   2. Information resources.   3. Electronic information resources.
4. Internet searching.   5. Electronic information resource searching.   6. Google.   I. Title.
ZA3075.M33 2012
001.4'2—dc23   2012010974

PRINTED IN THE UNITED STATES OF AMERICA

10 9 8 7 6 5 4

Most Prentice Hall Press books are available at special quantity discounts for bulk
purchases for sales promotions, premiums, fund-raising, or educational use. Special books, or
book excerpts, can also be created to fit specific needs. For details, write: Special Markets,
Penguin Group (USA) Inc., 375 Hudson Street, New York, New York 10014.

To Lisa

Of all the things I have found out over the years,
the one thing I learned that matters most is how lucky a guy I am.

Saber es poder.

CONTENTS

How to Think Like a Researcher

How much money does my boss make? Where is my great-grandmother buried? Who did my college girlfriend marry? How many other card stores are there in the town where I want to open mine? How can I change careers at the age of fifty? What companies would want to buy what my company produces and whom should we contact?

Welcome to the information age. Questions like these were once no more than things to ponder as you fell asleep, but now the answers are at the tips of your fingers—if you know where, and how, to look.

Research is the process of finding out for yourself what somebody else already knows. Every time you consult a book on how to cook a flounder filet or Google for information about your daughter's college or ask the advice of your doctor about that strange pain in your arm, you make the assumption that an answer to your question is out there. You assume that someone has written a cookbook or built a website or studied physiology thoroughly enough to correctly diagnose what ails you. Your instincts are right, because we live in the Information Age.

In our literate society, people record what they know. They research and publish books. They create websites. They tweet on Twitter. They write articles, make videos, and appear on TV. They store knowledge in their own heads. Information surrounds us as surely as water surrounds a fish, simply because someone decided to record what he or she knows. As evidenced by everything from ancient cuneiform writing pressed into clay tablets to the latest breaking news story online, humans need to put what they know into a form more permanent than speech. Whether the record is private, like a diary, or public, like a newspaper, ideas, thoughts, and data are stored in written form.

Paradoxically, for all the uncountable words and pictures we can conjure up with the click of a mouse, the Information Age poses it own unique problem: With so much information available, finding the useful fact or reliable study or collection of data to answer a question turns out to be more challenging than it seems, even with a powerful tool like Google to help us look.

This book will address the single most common misconception of the Information Age: that Google is the be-all and end-all of research. Speaking as a law librarian with more than twenty-five years in the research trenches, I can tell you that it isn't. Google has an important role to play in many research tasks, but it's only one tool of many that professional researchers rely on to get accurate and timely answers to thorny questions. It's ideal for many ordinary, humdrum tasks, like locating the address of a restaurant or finding out last night's baseball scores. The picture is much different, though, when we start to distinguish quick searches from serious research. Getting past a dependence on Google and other search engines is the focus of this book. As all good librarians know, there's a lot more useful information in the world than what search engines can deliver. And even on those occasions when Google is, in fact, the right tool to use, too many people overlook the powerful features of the "Advanced Search" option and instead muddle through with sloppy, bloated search results. There are better ways to find what you want.

Serious research is information gathering that is complex, demanding, and undertaken for a more critical purpose than finding out how tall your favorite celebrity is. For instance, you may be conducting research to flesh out a business proposal for a new company you want to set up in the solar power industry and need to find competitive intelligence. Or you might be a graduate student writing a paper on an emerging scientific subject like nanotechnology. Maybe you're putting together a family genealogy project and digging through historic records. In these instances, your research will require you to talk to experts, find books, or perform more in-depth research. The world of knowledge is a big one, and as I'll soon make clear, Google cannot see it all.

Complex research requires skill, imagination, and creativity. It's no longer the exclusive province of librarians and journalists. Any researcher—from students to scientists, journalists, and job seekers—whose curiosity ranges beyond simple searches will see just how much richer and more informative the online and print universe can be. This is something every student and professional needs to understand.

Most important, though, is learning how to think through a research problem. All questions, from the idly curious (Did that guy in eighth grade who played guitar ever make it as a musician?) to the academic (I need to create a comprehensive bibliography on all articles and books written about Renaissance painter Andrea del Verrocchio for a biography), can be approached the same way. Knowing how to work through a research problem will allow you to reliably find whatever it is that you need to know, be it frivolous or profound.

As you'll see, finding information is not a haphazard task; rather, it's an explicit process that has a beginning, a middle, and an end. Like any technique, it can be learned. Research techniques are dependable ways to bridge the gulf between knowing and not knowing. Whether you're nosing around your local town library to find a biography of your favorite writer or downloading giant data sets from a U.S. government agency or from a university in a remote country, the principles of research are the same. By mastering the research process and undertaking it in the spirit of adventure and discovery, you'll soon realize that it is indeed possible to find out anything.

The Process of Research

The first thing a researcher needs to learn is the art of crafting a question. This is where all good librarians begin their searches, and you should too. So let's plunge right in and start where most research ordinarily begins—the question itself.

Ask a Question That Can Be Answered

Philosopher Bertrand Russell said it best: "The greatest challenge to any thinker is stating the problem in a way that will allow a solution." Asking a question that can be answered is the greatest challenge that most researchers face too. If there's a single place where many otherwise bright and industrious people make a wrong turn when looking up information, it's at the very beginning of the research process. If you don't know what you are looking for, how will you know when you've found it?

But it's not enough merely to ask a question. You need to ask the right *kind* of question. Questions come in two varieties: open-ended and factual. The difference between the two is remarkable.

Open-ended questions ask for opinions and offer no definitive answer. Such questions, although frequently very interesting, do not readily allow for a solution. How would you come up with a definitive answer to such open-ended questions as, Is legalizing marijuana a good idea? Is Rome a better city for a vacation than Buenos Aires? Should the federal government spend more on the army than on education? As you can see, these questions open the door to discussion, but as far as getting to a concrete answer, they are impossible to work with.

Factual questions, by contrast, are answerable. For example, What is the population of Chicago? What drugs most prolong the life of a victim of cystic fibrosis? How many first dates does the average woman have in a lifetime?

Certainly many worthwhile research projects can arise from an intriguing but impossible-to-answer question. The conclusions that open-ended questions call for are great, but those conclusions can be drawn only after a steady accumulation of facts. More to our purpose, we need to ask answerable questions for the eminently practical reason that if a question has no end, neither does the research. Pursuing an open-ended question can be a fool's errand. So, to become a skilled researcher, step number one is learning how to craft the answerable question.

To become a skilled researcher, step number one is learning how to craft the answerable question.

Say you're a reporter for a business magazine and your editor wants to run an article on computer executive compensation. The editor asks you to find out if computer executives are overpaid. This is a great idea for a magazine article. It would probably make for a nifty feature in any number of business and tech magazines.

Your initial reaction might be to start Googling the question right away, and you type in "Are computer executives overpaid?" You would soon come up against some cold, hard truths. An open-ended question like that, which has no right or wrong answer, is not something that Google can wrestle with effectively. As we'll see, it's a simple finding aid, not the Oracle at Delphi. The question flunks the initial smell test for the simple reason that there is no *factual* answer to the question. What you or the editor might call *overpaid* would sound like peanuts to Bill Gates.

Not only does this question suffer from the crippling flaw of calling for an opinion, but it isn't well-defined. Exactly which executives are we talking about? CEOs? Financial officers? Head programmers? And which computer companies are we talking about? Would this be companies that design software, like Microsoft, or companies that retail computers, like Dell? In short, this question might be a plum assignment for a skilled reporter, but as far as an answerable question goes, it's worthless.

But don't throw your hands up in frustration and disgust just yet. Instead, let's recast that open-ended question into a series of factual questions that you *can* answer.

- How much did CEO Scott McNealy of Sun Microsystems earn in 2007?

- What was the average salary paid to the chief executive officers at the ten largest computer companies in the past five years?

- Who is an expert on computer industry compensation whom I can interview and quote?

- What books can I consult that discuss compensation trends in the software industry?

By coming up with a series of factual questions to ask, the initial abstract question starts to take shape as a concrete project. These factual questions will yield to diligent research because answers to each of them can be found. You now have a game plan. As I'll show in later chapters, you can answer these factual questions by searching public records databases, scrutinizing library catalogs, talking to associations, and conducting in-depth Google searches. For now, it is enough to know that successful research begins by asking not only the right questions but the right types of questions.

So how do you turn those hazy, unanswerable, open-ended questions into something you can work with? To determine exactly what someone is looking for, professional librarians conduct a *reference interview*. A reference interview is the formal process by which an answerable question is extracted from a general description of what a person is looking for. For a conscientious librarian, it's critical—failure to interview the patron properly can result in a waste of time and money. I know from personal experience. One afternoon, a lawyer called to ask me to send him a company's annual report, which I dutifully did. A few minutes later, he asked me to send him the company's proxy statement. Then, not long after, he asked for the company's quarterly report. Finally, he called me, the exasperation and frustration evident in his voice.

"Do me a favor," he said. "Find out who this company's general counsel is." Ah, so that's what he really wanted! The lawyer was asking for what he *thought* he needed—the annual report, the proxy, and the quarterly report—rather than for what he *actually* needed, which was a discrete piece of information contained in precisely none of the documents he asked me to send to him. (I found the answer in a book titled *The Directory of Corporate Counsel*.) Because I failed to have a reference interview in the beginning, I wasted both of our time. A ten-second interview would have prevented it.

Because you probably don't keep your own personal librarian on retainer, you need to learn to conduct a reference interview with yourself. The goal is to distill your initial curiosity into an action plan. Once you get the hang of it, you'll be able to quickly cut through the fog of open-ended questions to create a list of queries with definitive answers. As long as the questions you ask yourself begin with the words *what, when, where,* or *who*—the classic four Ws of journalism school, with the occasional addition of *how*—then you are well on the way to constructing questions that, when answered, might also illuminate the larger, open-ended question. Understanding precisely what you need to know is the difference between successful research and a never-ending slog through the back alleys of the Internet or the dusty shelves of libraries.

Understand the Scope of Your Research

After you've created your information shopping list, you need to decide how much of it you need. A research question can be as simple and quick to answer as, What is the formal name of China? (It's the People's Republic of China, according to the *CIA World Factbook*.) Or maybe you need complex, book-length research that requires locating specialized repositories of information, contact with experts, and reviews of obscure documents and publications, which may take months to compile. (You're writing a book on the invention of CT scanning for diagnostic imaging for use in the medical field.) Or maybe, as in many research projects, you'll need to dig through disparate information sources before you have enough facts gathered to create a coherent picture:

1. Who owned the building with the fire violations that burned down? (Search the city real estate records to find that Company X owned that building.)

2. Who owns Company X? (Look through state corporation records to discover that Jane Smith and Jack Johnson own Company X.)

3. How can I contact Jane Smith and Jack Johnson? (Start with the online telephone directory AnyWho and work from there.)

Repeat the process until you've found everything you want.

Assume you're about to do a sales pitch at a company to sell your new human resources (HR) software. You want to know something about the HR director before you meet her. Do you need to know every detail about her? Or is it sufficient to know only that she has worked at Amalgamated OmniCorp for ten years and that she holds an MBA from Wharton? If that's the case, then your research may be over once you've looked up her bio from standard business biography sources. But what if you want to hire her to be the head of your HR software sales department so that she can sell your wares to other HR directors? In that case, you'll want to know more about her—her former positions, perhaps her graduate school thesis, and presentations she has delivered at the annual conference for HR directors. Your research will broaden considerably, requiring many more queries in databases and generally taking longer than a simple bio request.

But what if, instead of wanting to hire her, you want to sue her because she bad-mouthed you and your company on a blog? In that case, you need to really turn over every rock in the public record, see quotes in the news, and make sure that any information that pertains to the lawsuit has been located. This biographical egg hunt now becomes a more extensive exercise in digging up details. Formulating factual questions is one step; knowing just how much information you need is another critical aspect of successful research.

> **Knowing just how much information you need is another critical aspect of successful research.**

Getting a handle on the scope of research delivers many benefits. It provides a way of limiting the time you spend looking for answers. It restricts research to a reasonable set of resources, and it can often reduce the costs associated with research when expensive commercial database searching is required. Shaping your work in this way—by including both answerable questions and an estimate of what types of information will be required for a complete and accurate answer—gives your project a structure and direction. Because you usually are tracking down information to use for another purpose, such as for inclusion in a report, an article, or a speech, you eventually need to finish the data gathering and put the information you have found to good use. Research needs to end. By knowing how much information you need, you'll also know when you're done. With practice, you'll hone your sense of how long and how deeply you need to sniff around for relevant information.

Consider the Best Places to Look

The fundamental question of where to look for the answers to your questions is not a new problem. In the 1700s, famed English essayist Dr. Samuel Johnson put it this way:

> Knowledge is of two kinds. We know a subject ourselves, or we know where we can find information upon it. When we enquire into any subject, the first thing we have to do is to know what books have treated of it.

Dr. Johnson's prescription still holds true. You can search for information yourself and read up on a subject, or you can look for a person or an organization who can deliver the information to you and interpret it. For instance, you could start searching for information on Crohn's disease to educate yourself on the disorder, or you could instead talk to your neighborhood gastroenterologist and ask him to explain the details of the disorder to you. Without making too much of this, think of research either as a way to dig up an answer by reading up on the subject yourself or as a process of finding the right person or organization to teach you what you need to know. So where is the best place to start to look? It all depends on the question.

Librarians approach a problem methodically by thinking of the broad subject category the topic fits into and then trying to figure out what type of resource would be required to arrive at a solution. This process of categorization is second nature to librarians. They routinely create taxonomies and get into the habit of listing topics hierarchically. Over the years, one's mind starts to function like the index of a book: It reflexively starts broadly, then drills down into the specifics. Let me illustrate.

Imagine you're the curator of an art gallery. You want to put together an exhibition and publication to show how photography has changed since the advent of the digital camera. But, alas, you need to do all the research for the show yourself. How would you figure out how to mount the show and how to gather information for the book that will accompany the exhibit?

Like many people, you might be tempted to Google the question How has photography changed since the advent of digital technology? (Try it!)

Here's what I found: Opinions from people who took time to respond to Yahoo! Answers, an article from the *Telegraph*, and a Wikipedia article edited by dozens of different contributors. Scattered among the Google search results are interesting articles from a site called Original Photography, an undated history from LoveToKnow "Photography," and instructions on how to crop pictures in Photoshop. The results are a mishmash, some new, some old, some insightful, some . . . not so much.

What you won't see are the things that would actually help you put together the show.

You should start, instead, by asking a series of factual questions: When was the digital camera invented? Which professional photographers used to photograph with film cameras and now shoot in digital? What companies produce digital cameras? What difference does it make if you produce a photo using software rather than a traditional chemical darkroom? What do experts in the field think about the shift from film to pixels?

The list of questions for your exhibit may be lengthy. But each question would imply a place to look for an answer. It would suggest a category. To an experienced librarian, thinking about how photography has changed is, more broadly, a question about art history. The nuts and bolts of digital camera manufacturing is company and product research, a subset of business research. And the differences between working in a chemical darkroom and Photoshop? That's a question that would require analysis by an expert.

Next, you start to narrow down the questions. Is this something that a reference book could answer right away? Or is this a question for which the answer is not so black and white and would require you to consult a treatise to answer? Maybe this question could be answered with a news search. Or perhaps this is such a sophisticated question that you would need to ask a trained expert for an opinion (and hope to get one for free!). Would a government website have this information? Or could a simple Google search turn up what you need? With experience, most good librarians know immediately where to look because the nature of the question suggests how to approach it. You can pick up the same skills with a bit of practice.

For your photography exhibit, start with the easy stuff: When was the digital camera invented? A Google search is good for this. In fact, About.com has a perfectly serviceable article by inventor and film maker Mary Bellis titled "History of the Digital Camera" that bubbles right to the top of the results list and will get you going.

The trickier questions are going to need more imagination to answer. This exhibition is, more broadly, an exercise in art history. So it would be worthwhile to find an art historian who specializes in digital photography. A library catalog search from any large library (like the Library of Congress) would be a great way to locate recent titles that talk about the changing face of modern photography.

Who produces digital cameras? Now we're shifting from art history to business research. We could look for the names of companies that produce digital cameras, but consider just how messy a process that would be. Observe the rule that professionals follow: Never compile information yourself if someone else has already done it. Putting together a list of manufacturers is exactly the type of information that a manufacturers association would collect and make public. Find the association for digital camera makers and ask them. In this case, PMA (formerly the Photo Marketing Association) might be a good source to ask.

Never compile information yourself if someone else has already done it.

What difference does digital make over the darkroom? You're going to need to interview some photographers for that one or find the work of someone who has already spoken to digital photographers.

Before you know it, you have in hand an entire dossier on your subject, drawn from a variety of sources. Unlike researchers of the past, we have a breathtaking selection of places in which to look for answers. Dr. Johnson had to rely on his own edification or his local library. Not us. The most extraordinary feature of the Information Age is the sheer volume of material available. Not only are we working on the shoulders of all the millions of books that have ever been written (and which are quickly entering the electronic universe themselves), but we have a vast amount of organized information to sift through. We can select from books or online magazines, blogs and emails, websites and printed encyclopedias. We can also make phone calls; send emails; and talk to friends, colleagues, and experts. How do we make sense of this immeasurably large infosphere so that we can pluck just what we need from it and not find ourselves wandering around lost in the Internet forever?

This book will provide the answer to the question "Where do I look?"

- **Search the deep web:** Chapter 2 provides a guide to the world of online databases that Google can't see and explains Google's considerable limitations.

- **Search with "Advanced Search" in Google:** Chapter 3 discusses how to use Google most effectively.

- **Search the library:** Chapter 4 explains the resources waiting for you at the library (and it's not just books and magazines).

- **Search reference resources:** Chapter 5 talks about the bountiful sources of factual information and how to take best advantage of them.

- **Search for association expertise:** Chapter 6 will show how to enlist the advice of experts who are connected to associations, societies, and other organizations.

- **Search for people:** Chapter 7 offers tips and techniques for finding information on people.

- **Search for company or business information:** Chapter 8 explores the world of company and corporate information.

- **Search the public record:** Chapter 9 discusses how to harvest factual data from government sources.

Depending on your question, you will start with one of these sources. Simple questions may yield to a proper Google search. Others may require contact with an expert or a call to an organization that specializes in your subject. Some subjects are a breeze to research: The answers to questions free from controversy and that have long been accepted as fact are easy to find in collections of reference materials. Things like the speed of light, the size of a standard baseball, or the date on which

Prohibition ended are always within reach. But more sophisticated questions sometimes require special education or training to answer coherently, and you will need to know who the experts are and how to contact them. For subjects that deal with abstract scientific ideas (quantum physics, advanced computer engineering, cosmology) or disciplines that require a significant fund of prior knowledge to understand (medicine, the law, high finance) the researcher without the appropriate background would be at a loss even to ask the right questions.

No matter where you decide to search first, you must be sure that you are dealing with reliable sources. The oldest joke in the research world is to tell a patron, "I can get it for you fast, cheap, and accurate. Pick two." Deciding where to look first also includes selecting a source that will provide accurate information. Finding reliable answers means finding reliable sources.

Don't take anything you read online at face value.

Don't take anything you read online at face value. These days, so-called content farms are pumping out articles and putative expert sites as a way to ensnare the unwary. Those hits mean advertising dollars, and the sites do not focus on the quality of the content. They are trying to turn a buck without regard to the accuracy of the information they serve up.

Traditional newspapers, broadcast news, and mainstream websites take pains to build their reputations for credibility. That's why they hire fact checkers and copy editors and reporters who take care to get their information straight. Respectable media organizations want to assure readers that their research is reliable. Reliability extends not only to media sources but to others that produce information, such as professional associations; companies; experts who write books; and research institutions that produce scientific, medical, political, or historical information.

Sources that strive for reliability freely admit when they are wrong and make corrections publicly. This is laudable; you should follow the same principle. The best way to do it is to find sources that have verifiable credentials in their subject area. How can you tell that your source is reliable? It deals in facts and makes clear that expressions of opinion are exactly that. ("The sun will rise at 6:12 on April 19, 2013, in New York" is a fact. "I think it's exciting that the sun rises in the morning" is an opinion.) Next, sources should have some authority to state whatever they are making pronouncements on. Unless your Uncle Morty is a trained meteorologist, when he says that it's going to rain next Tuesday, such apparent "fact" holds no water, but when the National Weather Service says it will, then the prediction takes on credibility. Likewise, your father, who raised three kids, may say that the best way to deal with a colicky baby is to give him sugar drops, whereas the Mayo Clinic may have other, more substantial ideas. And unlike your beleaguered Pops, the Mayo Clinic will cite its own sources, a practice that's an immediate tip-off that a source takes pains to back up its assertions. Good sources don't make things up, and they don't simply make a statement and expect the statement to be believed. Reliable sources understand that smart readers are skeptical readers; they anticipate challenges and give statements heft by providing background.

Closely related to reliability is attribution. You should be able to clearly back up your own fact gathering or conclusions with sources. The ability to *attribute* information to a source puts the burden for accuracy on the source. If you are researching information to make a persuasive argument in a sales pitch or to sway a jury, it's good to be able to point out that the information you're quoting comes from a reliable source. "According to the U.S. Census Bureau, more Americans are aged twenty-five to thirty-five today than any other age group" stands a better chance of convincing a reader that such a thing is true and accurate than does, "Somebody named Courtney on her blog says she believes half the people she meets are about to . . . OMG, turn thirty! And it's, like, half the world is between twenty-five and thirty-five."

Reliable information is as free from bias as possible. In a famous split-screen scene from Woody Allen's movie *Annie Hall*, Allen's character Alvy Singer is complaining to his therapist about his love life. To the question "How often?," Alvy says, "Hardly ever. Maybe three times a week." Meanwhile, Annie's shrink asks her the same question, to which she answers, "Constantly. I'd say three times a week." In this case, the facts are not in dispute but the interpretation of them certainly is. It's human nature to put your best spin on the available facts. A conscientious researcher, though, knows going in that almost every information source has a built-in bias. Be alert to the bias. As we'll see in Chapter 9, advocacy groups and associations are terrific resources, but it's no secret that they spin information in the best light for their own interests. When you're evaluating a resource, take into account the source's inevitable bias, even when it's presenting seemingly factual information.

> When you're evaluating a resource, take into account the source's inevitable bias, even when it's presenting seemingly factual information.

Double-sourcing is a way to check that information that appears to be solid actually is. The saying "A lie can travel halfway round the world while the truth is putting on its shoes" (attributed variously to both Mark Twain and Winston Churchill) is still true. Inaccuracies and falsehoods feed off themselves, like the canard that Mohawk Indian steelworkers work on high bridges and buildings because they are genetically unafraid of heights. (They're no more or less afraid than anybody else. Many Mohawks from New York State worked in high steel projects because their fathers, brothers, and cousins helped them get good-paying jobs in the industry, not because of some chromosomal quirk.) Correct information can be corroborated. What is true in one place should also be true in another place. It is not an opinion that the sky is blue; it's a fact—a fact as verifiable in Russia as it is in Uruguay and Canada.

Accurate information withstands scrutiny. The standard for scientific research is that experimental results need to be replicable. The laws of nature don't change. What happens in one lab ought to also occur in another, so long as the experimental conditions are the same. Likewise, facts are the same the world over. They don't require belief to be true. I can swear all day that the moon is made of blue cheese, but evidence from multiple sources such as NASA and satellite probes will tell me that the moon is indeed composed of rock, not Roquefort.

Think Like a Detective

Use What You Know Now to Find Out What You Need to Know Later

The root of the word *detective* is "detect," which means to "discover or determine the existence of." That's a fair way to think about research, too. The skills that a detective uses to solve a murder and the ones a researcher uses, in hot pursuit of a stray fact to seal a marketing pitch or to convince a skeptical editor, are fundamentally the same. A detective has a crime scene with certain clues right under her nose. A researcher has a world of books, websites, and people to search through.

**One of the best secrets of good research
is the ability to use one bit of information
to find even more information.**

The detective part of research is for many the most interesting and rewarding part of the process. Leveraging a bit of information is like a smart investment that turns $100 into $1 million. The excitement of research comes when a little bit of knowledge leads to even more, and one of the best secrets of good research is the ability to use one bit of information (or document or website or article or name) to find even more information. Even small research projects can grow quickly to encompass a much larger sphere of knowledge if you're going about things correctly. Because most researchers by nature are curious and engaged with the world of information, this is a very satisfying part of research. How do you play Sherlock Holmes without having to wear a ridiculous-looking hat and smoke a pipe? Try to make the following ways of looking at materials a habit:

Look at internal references: Footnotes, callouts, and references to other works are the hidden gems that researchers should read as closely as the primary text. Don't ignore them.

Take note of the credentials: If the person quoted in an article has an opinion that you either like, want to challenge, or need to learn more about, note his or her affiliation. You might find additional information on the person's company, university, or association site.

Check the other links: Most websites and blogs offer additional links or blog rolls. Check them out. If the webmaster sees value in adding a link, there likely is something of value to you in following it.

Always ask for more information: Whether you are speaking to a person face-to-face or are engaged in an email conversation, never fail to ask where else you should be looking for additional information. People love to talk; you'll find that asking for advice can produce tips for finding more information quickly.

Stay Organized

Perhaps you're well organized by nature. If so, send me your secret, because I would love to naturally keep my information neat and easy to find. Judging by the appearance of many offices I visit, many other people also suffer from the heartbreak of disorganization.

The grand bazaar of information is worthless if you collect stuff and then just randomly stick it someplace. If you misplace the URL that held the exact quote you need to bolster your regulation of ostrich farms campaign or if you forget to write down the name of that nice lady from the Federal Aviation Administration who can answer all your questions about the number of failed front landing gear incidents for commercial jets that your client wants, you doom yourself to repeating work or to losing the benefit of your fine research efforts.

Get into the habit of keeping copious notes. Phone numbers, names, websites, stray facts...anything that may come in handy later. Write it all down or type it all into your computer. You'll save yourself time, effort, and frustration in the future.

Use Your Common Sense

Young doctors in training are taught "When you hear hoofbeats, think horses, not zebras." This advice goes for research, too. You don't need to search under every single rock for every single question. Most questions have straightforward answers, and often knotty questions turn out not to be as tough as you have made them out to be. By relying on common sense, you will learn how to save hours of research time. If a single website among millions says that Abraham Lincoln was shot at the Forge Theater or that the drummer for the Beatles was named Ring-o Star, you don't need to go nuts trying to see if any standard histories or encyclopedias agree. Common sense can tell you the site is wrong or suffers from a typo or a dozing copy editor.

Get off the Computer and Talk to People

Clearly, there is a virtually limitless expanse of information on the Internet. The web, though, merely added, admittedly in a very big way, to the tools that researchers of the past had been using. Those tools have not gone away. The telephone, mail, talking with colleagues and friends, phone books, old archives, and library gumshoeing are still great ways to mine information. In many instances, the fastest and most effective way to track down what you need to know is by picking up the telephone.

Resist the urge to Google everything. As you'll see in the next chapter, not only is Google quite limited in the information that it can provide but a strict reliance on Google cuts you off from the expertise of people with whom you can have a conversation. Picking up the phone to speak with the right person can sometimes get you an answer faster than even the fastest computer can.

Admittedly, Google is a very useful tool for finding phone numbers of people who might be able to answer questions, but so too are the online phone books I'll talk about in Chapter 7. I'll go into much more detail about finding experts and taking advantage of the specialized knowledge available from associations in later chapters, but the message here is that information gathering isn't solely about digging up data online. It also means making phone calls, visiting physical libraries, and corresponding by both electronic and snail mail.

Require Proof

Fact-Check Yourself

When you're looking for information, keep in mind that everything is guilty until proven truthful. Skepticism (not cynicism) is the ally of the researcher. You should always weigh the credibility of any source in light of what you already know and never take a fact, opinion, or conclusion at face value until you can verify it. Remember the old reporter's adage "If he says his mother loved him, check it out with her." Healthy skepticism requires proof; misinformation is more common than the truth.

> **Skepticism (not cynicism) is the ally
> of the researcher.**

Double-sourcing is always a good idea. This is the simple process of seeing if reputable sources agree on the facts. It should be fairly easy to verify that President Abraham Lincoln was in fact born on February 12, 1809, by checking standard American histories, reading biographies of Lincoln, or consulting an official Lincoln source such as the Abraham Lincoln Presidential Library. Things get tough when the information you need to verify is neither that cut-and-dried nor that easy to pinpoint.

Consider the conventional wisdom that holds that male-pattern baldness skips a generation. True or false? If you Google the question "Does baldness skip a generation?" you'll have no problem finding a variety of opinions on the matter. What you might have a problem with is discerning which of the very confident-sounding websites are publishing accurate information and which are peddling hooey. The skeptical mind will resist the charmingly ill-informed answers that bubble to the top of the Google results list from such pungently fact-free sites as Yahoo! Answers—"Yes, it can skip generations, several sometimes" is one opinion proffered by the esteemed expert named "Answerer 1"—and instead gravitate to sites with some semblance of credibility, like the Mayo Clinic, the National Institutes of Health, or PubMed from the National Library of Medicine. The National Library of Medicine's take on the question says, "The inheritance pattern of androgenetic alopecia (aka male-pattern baldness) is unclear because many genetic and environmental factors are likely to be involved. This condition tends to cluster in families, however, and having a close relative with patterned hair loss appears to be a risk factor for developing the condition."

Which source would you trust?

Assume Nothing

You and I have heard what assuming makes us. It's true. The smart researcher doubts everything and assumes nothing. The only worthwhile exception to this rule is to assume that an answer to your question exists and that if you follow the correct steps for research, you will find it.

Never Give Up

They didn't nickname the lions in front of the New York Public Library on Fifth Avenue Patience and Fortitude for nothing. Tenacity is as much a tool of successful research as curiosity and intelligence. Sticking to the task is important. There are times when locating a needed piece of information is, frankly, tough and tedious and the information you are looking for is as elusive as a hat blowing down the sidewalk in a windstorm. Research to turn up a critical piece of information may take many online searches or hours spent sifting through multiple documents, websites, or volumes in the library. Continuing in the face of frustration is as important a research skill as correctly framing your initial question.

> **Tenacity is as much a tool of successful research as curiosity and intelligence.**

Maybe you need to call around to government agencies or to professional associations. I can vouch that it will take at least thirteen transfers before you're finally connected to the right person. Maybe you need to locate a specific website for a very distinct product. Trust me, you'll visit a dozen of them before you settle on the right one. There's no getting around it: Research requires patience. Not all of the world's answers are at the end of a Google search. As a research project unfolds, you will hit dead ends. A magazine article that took three days to find and that promised to reveal exactly how Jell-O was invented turns out to be nothing more than a collection of recipes with no insight into the birth of Jell-O at all. A book that should have explained Robert E. Lee's thinking about his ultimately doomed military strategy at Gettysburg winds up being factually suspicious and amateurishly written. Or a website you hoped would provide scientific data needed to flesh out your proposal for sending a manned mission to Mars hasn't been updated in seven years. These types of strikeouts are common. Don't let them stop you. The real-world process of research is more of a bumpy road than the smoothly flowing superhighway that the early hype of the Internet promised.

It's tempting to think of today's information-drenched world as an ever-ripe garden overflowing with easy pickings. That's true in a limited way, but plucking the valuable data is not always so simple. Experienced researchers know that valuable information needs to be tracked down and is always more elusive than it seems at the outset. Researchers need to bring their own judgment to the task, evaluating sources and testing the information they find to make sure it's accurate and that it answers the question being asked. And as I've emphasized, information comes not just from a simple Internet search but from research into books, questions asked of experts, and commercial services that provide access to information. Like diamonds, answers rarely appear in front of you, shiny, complete, and fully formed. Instead, answers to questions are formed from the slow accretion of facts that yield a coherent story when piled one on top of another.

Researchers should heed Winston Churchill: "Never give in, never,

never, never, never, in nothing great or small, large or petty, never give in except to convictions of honour and good sense." Of course, when Churchill made this speech at the Harrow School in 1941 he was facing down the Wehrmacht, which is not something the average librarian has to do at work every day, but his point is well taken. Plugging along pays off, whether you are defending England against the Nazi hordes or tracking down the total gross sales of linoleum in 1968. Stick to it. You will find your answer.

Now let's take a look at the tools to help you do just that.

Google and the
Deep Web

Google

Google needs no introduction, but it certainly needs an explanation.

Google is a paradox. Without it, the Internet is nothing more than an incomprehensible jumble of websites, but, believe it or not, Google actually misses more information than it finds. This indispensable research tool cannot make sense of all the information stored in the recesses of the "deep web," a universe of databases where more information lives than in the "surface web" that Google users can see. Google makes the keyword search box so trivially simple to use, most users overlook the far more powerful "Advanced Search," which can produce much better search results. Users tolerate the truckloads of useless information that every broad Google search turns up when they could save themselves time and effort by learning how to filter their results. And technology aside, Google's seeming omnipotence lulls researchers into thinking that they've exhausted the known universe of information when, in fact, they've merely generated a crowd-sourced list of suggested places to look. Google is the Schrödinger's cat of search engines—it's simultaneously the greatest boon to online research ever invented and the archnemesis of effective information gathering.

Google, of course, is not the only search engine in town, but it is by far the best known and most powerful; according to Search Engine Watch, an organization that tracks such things, more than two thirds of all search engine queries each month are run on Google, so I'll limit my discussion to it alone. For our purposes, which is learning how to conduct serious research, we need to understand three critical things about the Internet's number-one search tool:

- It cannot yet comprehensively search the deep web (sometimes called the "invisible web") and so misses more than it finds;

- Users don't use "Advanced Search" and consequently suffer with bloated search results;

- Google is great for simple searches, but users too often accept Google's results at face value without critically evaluating what they are seeing.

It's this last item that should concern us most. We'll get up to speed on the deep web shortly, and all of Chapter 3 is devoted to learning "Advanced Search." Before we get to those, it's important to understand that Google works best when you bring your own judgment to the process. The old teacher's chestnut, "You get out of it what you put in to it" applies here too. And in fact it was a history teacher, Kevin M. Levin, who summed up the problem with Google perfectly when he described how his students approached online research. In the *New York Times*, he wrote,

> These days, children turn first to their search engines to find information; they conduct a few keyword searches and click on the most popular results without questioning either the search engine's ranking algorithm or the source of the content.... A search is only as good as the search strategy. The outcome of any search will be determined by a host of factors, including the choice of browser and keywords.

Levin is on to something. Popping a few words into Google and taking what comes back as gospel is a sketchy proposition. He's not the only one who worries that online users are uncritical consumers of search engine results. In 2008, the British Library and the Joint Information Systems Committee (JISC) studied the so-called Google generation to find out how effectively people were using new technology tools to look up and read information. In the report titled "Information Behaviour of the Researcher of the Future," the library concluded that more time is spent browsing the web than critically evaluating information. At the risk of sounding like some hectoring schoolmaster, what Google has done is to make it easier to skim a wide variety of information. It does not encourage a deep dive into the text. That's a problem.

If a steady diet of junk food and a sedentary lifestyle leads to flabbiness, an unvaried diet of search engine results (accepting Google abstracts as writ without critical reading) leads just as surely to something that James Morris, former dean of the School of Computer Science at Carnegie Mellon, calls "infobesity." Half-baked explanations, errors in facts or logic, and other unfiltered detritus that Google unearths can make for easy access to inaccurate information. Just because the text was produced by some fancy computer program and is displayed on a sleek tablet computer does not make the text any more or less reliable. A skeptical engagement with search results is as important as the analysis a smart reader would apply to the text of a traditional book.

> **Just because the text was produced by some fancy computer program and is displayed on a sleek tablet computer does not make the text any more or less reliable.**

So, with all due deference to its undeniably brilliant engineering, Google is fundamentally a web-indexing tool. We need web-indexing tools, of course, the same way books need tables of contents and indices. Strangely, while no one would seriously argue that looking over the table of contents and the index of a book is the same as reading the whole work, too many Google users think it's fine to skim the results list and stop there, which is essentially the same thing. And when well-written and reasoned materials appear right next to things that could have been written by a trained ape, it can be easy to give them equal weight: Many Google users conclude that whatever sites make the cut and show up within the all-important top twenty results are of equal value, and that just isn't necessarily so.

> **Online information should go through the same critical vetting process material does in print.**

Online information should go through the same critical vetting process material does in print. Does this author know what the heck she is talking about? Is this information accurate? Is it free from bias? If the author is making a point, does the reasoning hold up or does the author make specious claims? Has care been taken to write clearly and grammatically? In short, reading through a list of Google results is first and foremost an exercise in making choices about which results promise to answer your questions and which should be dismissed as unworthy of your attention. It is a given that Google will produce far more results than you could ever possibly need—it is up to you to sift through this mass and find the materials that contain valuable information.

Of course, Google occupies a very important place in your arsenal of tools to help you find out anything. It exists to point you to the places where you need to look for information. It does an excellent job of that, but even then, bear in mind that Google suffers from a giant blind spot concerning the deep web. The term *deep web* refers to the universe of web-accessible information locked away in databases where Google's spidering computers can't see it. That limitation is a very serious knock against Google and the most important reason for never depending on it exclusively for online information.

The Deep Web

In the 1990s, information professionals began to notice a peculiarity about search engines. Most did a credible job of locating web pages when all of a site's information was readily exposed. (Remember, this was back in the days when most websites presented their information on web pages built from flat HTML, not the fancy, feature-rich sites we see today.) Web design matured. Most sites were designed to pull information from a database. No longer were sites created from hard-coded text. Instead, they produced information on the fly, pulled from a database, in response to user queries. Suddenly, search engines didn't look as omnipotent as they once did. These days, the bulk of the interesting data is in the database, not on a web page where Google's computers can find it.

Look at it this way. You certainly can Google the question "Do any trains run between Philadelphia and Boston on July 19?" Google obligingly finds more than 1,900,000 possible responses to the question. But, really, what you want to do is go to Amtrak's site; specify the time, date, and class of service; and generate an answer from a database. By querying the Amtrak trip planner, you are tapping into the deep web. Or you may Google all you want for available tickets to the Bruce Springsteen concert, but eventually you'll need to go to StubHub! or eBay or TicketMaster to run a search, because Google can't peek into the database to see if the tickets are available. Deep web again. And this is the crux of the issue. Using Google for simple and routine questions is fine, but for academic research, in-depth business searches, tracking down people, or locating historic or hard-to-find data, Google searching doesn't cut it. You have to know how to wring answers out of the deep web if you want to do thorough research. That will mean time spent searching databases, following the leads suggested by those databases, and digging around on searchable pages to find information.

> **For academic research, in-depth business searches, tracking down people, or locating historic or hard-to-find data, Google searching doesn't cut it.**

Imagine you are a graduate student in art history writing a paper about the American photographer Timothy O'Sullivan. When I ran a Google search, I found a Wikipedia page, a guide to his work from the J. Paul Getty Museum, something from a website called Masters of Photography, and a whopping three paragraphs from the *Encyclopaedia Britannica* along with more than 100,000 other hits, including pictures, YouTube videos, and plenty of links to other Timothy O'Sullivans, very few of whom photographed the Gettysburg battlefield. Do you stop with that Google search? Of course not. Google is a great tool to use to start research, but it's a terrible place to end it. The smart researcher realizes that the really useful information is hidden away in databases that you'll need to seek out yourself. Think of the questions that Google is *not* answering. Where in that results list is the bibliography of scholarly articles about his work? Did it name the experts in nineteenth-century Civil War photography? What do current photo collectors think of O'Sullivan's work? How much are his pictures worth? And where would you go, as an ambitious grad student, to see for yourself what the original pictures looked like?

For those answers, you'll need to leave the confines of Google and start plugging queries into art history databases, mining library catalogs with extensive holdings in photography, and maybe even paying a small subscription fee to one of the commercial services that track sales prices in the art market. This heavy lifting is for you to do, not Google. If what you most want to see is deep in a database, it won't bubble up in a hit list.

As you work through your research questions, you will discover that your answer will lie not in the contents of web pages that Google can see but in the searchable databases that it can't. These databases account for far more information than anything that is readily visible on the so-called surface web. And it is these databases and their contents are the bread and butter of good research. Let Google or the deep web search engines find the databases for you, and then search the appropriate ones for the question you're asking.

Searchable databases and their contents are the bread and butter of good research.

Although the numbers from the experts are always inexact, the deep web is estimated to contain at least *four or five times* the amount of information that sites publish directly to the web and that is available to Google and other search engine. This tip-of-the-iceberg picture means that any conscientious researcher ought to be focusing on the retrievable data from the databases of the deep web more than on the results of a simple Google search.

Although I am not a fan of Wikipedia for research, I will in this one instance recommend it for its ongoing description of the invisible web as a way to keep up with developments in the area. Search engine companies, Google especially, understand that the current inability to harvest the riches of the hidden web is a significant handicap and are working to solve the problem. Wikipedia, if it is working as intended, should stay on top of developments. If you're interested in the topic, I also recommend Search Engine Watch, which keeps an eye on the latest technology news about search engines.

Mining the Deep Web

Just because Google can't do a deep dive into the vast underground stores of information doesn't mean the riches of the deep web are off-limits to you. Quite the contrary. The immense repositories of facts, data elements, and information are eminently searchable, assuming that the sites that store information don't restrict access. The value of the deep web is important enough that specialized search engines have cropped up to compete with the almighty Google.

IncyWincy

IncyWincy, the self-described "Invisible Web Search Engine," provides a unique window into the hidden world of online databases. IncyWincy focuses its search power on locating websites that are equipped with queryable databases. The IncyWincy "Forms" search provides you with an easy way to locate websites that contain one or more search forms, which usually indicates that a database cannot be far away. For example, searching for "coal" on the IncyWincy "Forms" tab will return a list of web pages containing a search form. In this example, you will be able to dig through the databases of the World Coal Institute, the Coal Utilization Research Council, the American Coalition for Clean Coal Electricity, and more, from a single web page.

INFOMINE

INFOMINE is an excellent resource for scholarly materials, fashioned by academic librarians from the University of California. According to INFOMINE, the search engine digs through "useful Internet resources such as databases, electronic journals, electronic books, bulletin boards, mailing lists, online library card catalogs, articles, directories of researchers, and many other types of information."

DeepPeep

DeepPeep is figuring out how to use a single search page to search multiple databases. It has identified more than 45,000 web forms to allow instant retrieval from automobile, airfare, hotel, and job sites.

These all are the type of web pages that require a user to know some search parameters, like date, prices, and destinations, to produce meaningful results. The answers DeepPeep dredges up are interesting, but they haven't quite cracked the deep web nut just yet.

If you're interested in learning more about the deep web, try Bright Planet, a company that has pioneered identification of the features of the deep web and is devising a means to exploit it. Although Google cannot search the deep web, its "Advanced Search" can be an important tool for finding the databases that will lead you there, as you'll see in the next chapter.

SITES AND SOURCES MENTIONED IN THIS CHAPTER

Amtrak
www.amtrak.com

Bright Planet
http://brightplanet.com

DeepPeep
www.deeppeep.org

eBay.com
www.ebay.com

Google
www.google.com

IncyWincy
www.incywincy.com

INFOMINE
http://infomine.ucr.edu

"Information Behaviour of the Researcher of the Future"
www.jisc.ac.uk/media/documents/programmes/reppres/ggworkpack ageii.pdf

StubHub!
www.stubhub.com

"Teaching Civil War History"
http://opinionator.blogs.nytimes.com/2011/01/21/teaching-civil-war-history-2-0

TicketMaster
www.ticketmaster.com

U.S. Government Printing Office
www.gpoaccess.gov

Wikipedia
www.wikipedia.com

The Ins and Outs
of Google

The "Advanced Search" Template

The tools of Google's "Advanced Search" deliver the holy grail of search results—namely, a small number of highly relevant hits. Since the average Google search routinely returns an absurd number of hits, getting your list whittled down to a manageable scale is a necessity for the busy researcher. "Advanced Search" is how we force Google to be more precise.

> **"Advanced Search" is how we force
> Google to be more precise.**

The supersize results list that Google produces from a keyword search is no accident. The programming is designed to be all-inclusive;

the search rules cast a wide net in an effort not to miss anything. That's a worthy goal, but let's face it: After you've looked at the first 25 hits, interest in the remaining 1,256,897 fizzles pretty quickly. Think of how much easier it would be to put your finger on exactly what you're looking for if the list you were working with were both shorter and better tailored to your needs. Any home chef who has ever reduced stock will understand the principle: Boil things down to the essence. That's what "Advanced Search" does.

Using "Advanced Search" to manage a lengthy results list is a two-step process. First, ask a better question—better questions come from using syntax tools to formulate better queries. Second, you'll need to reduce the number of web pages that Google consults to create your hit list by using the filter tools to exclude things you don't need to see. When used together, better queries and sensible filtering will not only chop your results list down to a reasonable size but greatly improve the informational signal-to-noise ratio. Remarkably, Google reports that fewer than 5 percent of all searchers, including Google's own staff, use these tools. That's a shame. They're easy to master, and they supercharge your search results.

The link to the "Advanced Search" template lives underneath the gear tool that you will find after you have run an initial search. Learn where the link lives and make the "Advanced Search" template your starting point for all Google searching from this point forward. After you see how much better your results become, you can wean yourself from the "Advanced Search" template and instead get the same great results by typing out all the shortcuts directly into the standard search box on Google's home page.

The search template, like most things Google designs, is a marvel of concision. The top four text boxes are the syntax tools that help you ask a better question. Below the syntax tools are the filters that pare down results list dramatically. These filters include the most useful tool in the bunch, the site or domain restrictor. The last two, the "Page-Specific Tools," are two services that depend directly on Google's celebrated PageRank system. When you find a page or site that speaks directly to your question and then want to find more pages just like that one, these services will locate additional pages or sites similar to the pertinent one you've found.

I recommend following along on your own computer as we tour the features of "Advanced Search."

The Syntax Tools

Professional researchers trained on commercial search databases like Nexis, Dow Jones News Service, Dialog, or Factiva normally construct searches using Boolean connectors. This is the formal name for describing how a researcher can tell a database, "Show me this, but not that." We emulate this in Google by specifying words we want to include, words we want to exclude, which words need to be treated as a single concept, and, at times, which different words are okay to search simultaneously because we'd be happy with results containing any one of them.

> **TEXT BOX:** all these words
> **SYMBOL:** quotation marks [" "]
> **TOOL:** Google Verbatim

One of the reasons the average Google keyword search returns so many results is that the search engine looks not only for your term but for synonymous terms as well. In a keyword search, Google takes your search term, associates it with similar words and then returns that monster list, bloated with links to pages about which you could not care less. To get around Google's noble attempt to be all-inclusive and instead make it more precise, put your keyword in quotation marks. This tells Google to dispense with the synonyms and deliver pages containing just your actual word or words, starting with pages in which your term is in the title of the page, the URL of the page, or, ideally, in both places. Given that well-designed websites will usually contain meaningful words in their URLs or the names of their pages, the most relevant matches should naturally bubble to the top. Shutting off the synonyms will confer immediate benefits in more precise results. I recommend using it for every search.

Old-time Google users once used the plus sign (+) for the same purpose, but with the advent of the social networking site Google+, the plus sign has been kicked upstairs and now serves not as a search operator but as a brand mark. To replace the plus sign, Google introduced Google Verbatim in the autumn of 2011: Run a search and then select Google Verbatim from the list of "More Search Tools." Google will indulge you by looking for precise, literal matches to your search words. For experienced searchers, this ability to select exact words or phrases is a godsend. While it's true that plain keyword searching without any punctuation does a serviceable job of returning relevant results, smart researchers benefit from more control of Google queries when using the quotation marks.

> ## Smart researchers benefit from more control of Google queries when using the quotation marks.

Quotation marks also come in handy when searching for something that requires two or more words to express. Quotes around a search phrase tell Google to search for the phrase as a single concept and not as multiple isolated words.

"French poodle"

"Barack Obama"

"intellectual property law"

"cat lady" "The Simpsons"

"database" "interest rates"

"search" "baby names"

One caution, though. The quotation marks around a phrase are taken quite literally by Google. The phrase "John Kennedy" is a unique search and will not directly include "John F. Kennedy Jr." The quotation marks tell Google to look for only those exact terms. "New York City" is a different search from "NY City" and "NYC." The quotation marks are a powerful tool, so use them judiciously.

TEXT BOX: But don't show pages that have . . .
SYMBOL: minus sign (hyphen) [-]

The power to say no is a very useful one. It really comes in handy in the Googlesphere, where adding a simple minus sign (type a hyphen) to a search term is the way to exclude that term from the query. In a language like English, in which a single word can have many different meanings, it's critical to be able to explain which sense of the word you don't want Google to search. Consider what would happen if you Googled for "avatar" in hopes of learning about Hindu mythology, but had no interest at all in the movie about the blue people. The power to elegantly exclude the millions of references to the film makes it much easier to find the avatar contexts that you *do* want to see. See it in action by first Googling for

"Avatar"

Look at the curiously bracing number of results Google delivers. Now watch what happens when a little bit of exclusion works its magic. Compare the sheer number of results you get when you search:

"Avatar" -movie

That little minus sign (hyphen) slays a horde of a billion or more false hits. Formally speaking, the minus sign helps disambiguate results. Informally, we can call it uncluttering results by getting rid of false hits. When your search term has more than one meaning, use the minus sign to knock out meanings you don't want from the results list:

That little minus sign (hyphen) slays a horde of a billion or more false hits.

"Newt" -Gingrich

"water table"-restaurant

"space planning" -NASA -"outer space" -rockets

TEXT BOX: one or more of these words
CONTROL: OR
SYMBOL: pipe symbol [|]

46

In Googlespeak, a space between search terms is always inter-preted as the word *and*. The following Google search:

"dalmatians" -Disney -101

tells Google, "Find me the exact word *Dalmatians* in the title or the URL of a web page AND exclude the word *Disney* AND exclude the number *101*." What about those times when you want to search for two or more different things at the same time, but you don't need for the search terms to appear together? This is handy for those times when you can't decide what to make for dinner or which camera to buy:

"Recipe" "lasagna" OR "lobster bisque" OR "chicken soup"

"digital SLR" "Nikon" | "Canon" | "Leica"

Other Syntax Tools

Certain syntax tools have a symbol, but they don't have a correspond-ing search box on Google's "Advanced Search" template. Don't hesi-tate to use them as needed.

Asterisk
An asterisk acts as a wild card, inviting Google to fill in the blank:

SYMBOL: asterisk [*]

"IBM" "incorporated" state of *

"King * of Jordan"

* a cold * a fever

An asterisk acts as a wild card, inviting
Google to fill in the blank.

Brackets

When you want to search for a phrase or word that contains a punctuation mark or word that might be construed as a search symbol,
like a hyphen or the word *or*, place the search term in brackets. Using
brackets tells Google to treat what's inside (punctuation, a word, a
symbol) literally and to search for it in results.

A phrase containing the operator "OR" can be searched literally:

SYMBOL: brackets [[ ]]

[to be or not to be]

[give me liberty or give me death]

Going All In

In addition to searching for text that appears on a web page, some
very handy search controls can look for your search term in a specific
place *in* a web page: its title, its URL, or the anchor tag (which most
people call a "link").

Search for a single word in any of these places by using the commands as shown in these examples:

inurl:chevrolet

intitle:longfellow

inanchor:combustion_engine

Similarly, find multiple words in any of these places by using the "allin" control—no quotation marks required:

allinurl:felony defense

allintitle:Jackson snakes plane

allintext:bedbugs remedy

And there you have it. The minus sign (hyphen), quotation marks, asterisk, and the word *OR* plus a handful of other syntax tools will help narrow your search. These symbols and controls are the first of the two steps on your way to transforming your Google results from a "before" picture to an "after."

Now that you've learned how to ask Google better questions, let's next see how to cut the web down to size.

Web Filters

Deliberately dumb rhetorical question: Do you need to search every web page on earth every time you want to find out the capital of Nebraska? I'm guessing not. Part two of our exercise in slimming down the hit list is the use of search filters that either automatically exclude certain types of information or focus the search on specific web pages. Some of these filters cut your results list down to size *before* you search; others, like the date restriction, wield their knife after you've gotten back a set of results. For example, you can restrict results by date using the "Advanced Search" template before you hit the "Search" button. When you search from the

Google home page, however, you'll need to filter by date after the results have appeared.

Domain and Site Searching

Of all the tools Google provides to help you search the web, none is as powerful or as useful as the site/domain search. Say you want to get information about diabetes research, but you want the information to come only from official U.S. government sites.

> Of all the tools Google provides to help
> you search the web, none is as powerful
> or as useful as the site/domain search.

Without recourse to the domain filter, you could spend the better part of an afternoon trying to pluck out the government materials from the hot mess of links to universities, personal websites, content farms, peddlers of quack cures, and the like. Instead, you can restrict your search to government sites very elegantly by searching like this:

"diabetes" site:.gov

"search" "gasoline prices" site:.gov

The top-level domains of the Internet should be familiar to all web users by now. Commercial sites are in the .com domain, schools and universities are in the .edu domain, U.S. government sites are .gov, and nonprofits are .org. All the nations of the world have been assigned a two-letter domain of their own: .ca (Canada), .mx (Mexico), .ch (Switzerland, for the Cantons Helvetica), .th (Thailand), and so on.

The complete list of top-level domains is found at the Internet Corporation for Assigned Names and Numbers (ICANN), the agency that sets the Internet's addressing standards.

Want only French sites? Try adding site:.fr to your search. Just need academic sites? Then site:.edu will do the trick. Whatever the domain, the site: filter will search it. Conversely, to exclude results from a particular domain, add a minus sign (hyphen) as in the following examples:

> "admissions" "Yale" site:.edu -site.com (finds Yale University, not Yale Locks)

> "charity" "adoption" site:.org -site:.gov (finds organizations, not government sites)

Searching a Specific Website

As convenient as it is to limit Google to a specific high-level domain, forsaking all others, perhaps my favorite filter of all is the site restrictor. This essentially uses Google to search a specific site. When you consider how many menus and levels and irrelevant pages you usually have to slog through to find that choice piece of information on most complex websites, this is one of the handiest tools to have at your disposal. Because most sites have flabby, low-power, built-in search boxes and elaborate menu systems that suck up time as you try to find something, having a way to use Google to reach inside a website and pull back exactly what you need is ideal. Why knock yourself out plowing through complex websites or sifting through results lists when you can jump right to the good stuff? Say you need to fast-shop the Tiffany site for a necklace or look for the chemical properties of ruthenium from the American Chemical Society or find the in-state tuition for Oregon State University? Don't muck around with the search boxes on the respective sites. Do it the easy way, like this:

"necklace" site:tiffanys.com

"ruthenium" site:acs.org

"tuition" "in-state" site:oregonstate.edu

Of all of Google's powers, I have found nothing will make your online search better faster than using domain and site restrictions. Once you make domain searching a habitual part of your Google search creation, you'll spend more time finding and less time searching. It's a terrific feature. Along with quotation marks and the hyphen, use the site: feature whenever you can.

Of all of Google's powers, nothing will make your online search better faster than using domain and site restrictions.

Date Restrictions

For the casual Google user, a search result list is a crazy quilt of information, with results pulled from all over the calendar. A typical list has links to websites where one result might have been updated yesterday, the next one last December, and the one after that six years ago. Sort out the snarl with Google's time tools. To access the service, run a search and then click "More Search Tools" on the left-hand side of the page. The drop-down menu will reveal the options for filtering your search results by time—from past hour to past year, including a custom range. The date filter is a godsend for the researcher who needs to look for a news story or a web page containing time-sensitive information. This is a frequently overlooked tool. You can restrict the date before you search by using the "Date" drop-down menu in Google's "Advanced Search" template to select your range. But if you are searching from the main page, run your search and then select from the date restrictors.

> **The date filter is a godsend for the researcher who needs to look for time-sensitive information.**

Language

I say tomato, you say *il pomodoro*. The web is global. So is Google. Search sites for whatever language your *petit coeur* desires, and the language tool will bring back your answers in the selected tongue. Note that the heavy-duty language search—in which Google will take your English-language query, translate it into another language, search sites in that language, and then return you a list of results translated from that language into English, lives in the "Language Tools" feature, a fancy tool that can be found in the drop-down menu when you click on the gear icon. More on that in a moment.

File Type

In those instances when you know that the information you want will be in a specific format—a court decision in pdf format or a professor's presentation in PowerPoint, for instance—it pays to search not for a website but for a specific document format. This feature is not widely used, but I have found it to be useful when querying for materials that would most likely live on a spreadsheet, such as a list or financial data.

The control is named filetype: and can be used in a search string, as follows:

"Roe v Wade" filetype:pdf (pdf file)

"SuperBowl winners" filetype:xls (Microsoft Excel file)

"sales" " motivation" filetype:ppt (Microsoft PowerPoint presentation)

Where Your Keywords Show Up

Keyword location allows you to find sites where your search term appears on a page title, in a URL, in the text of the page, or in links to the page from other sites. This feature helped a trademark researcher I know who was trying to find websites that were selling unlicensed merchandise that infringed on a client's trademarks. To find sites that have used a trademark without permission in their URLs, conduct a Google search with the command inurl:. If the trademark were XYZ, then you would search for inurl:XYZ. Once my friend had the search results, he was able to track down the owners of those sites (using domain registration information) fairly quickly.

Google normally searches everywhere on a web page, but you can direct the search engine to focus on the title of a page, the URL, or the text a page when needed. Common sense says that any web page in which *marktwain* appears in the URL will probably have something to do with the author.

Region

The region search is simply a twist on the domain restriction. A region search uses the two-letter country code for each nation of the world to limit online scrutiny to that country's online contents. Like the example above, a region-restricted search is just a convenient way of fencing in your results lists to pages from a certain country. If the guacamole recipes you're searching for just have to come from a source in Mexico, select it from this pulldown list, or use the afore-mentioned domain restriction and type out site:.mx. Either way, you get the same results.

Numeric Range

To look for prices within a range of values, use the numeric range control. You can type out a range in the main Google search box using two periods to separate the values, as in the following searches:

"car" "used" $5000..$8000

"shoes" "Louboutin" $250..$500

Page-Specific Tools

If, in the course of your research, you hit upon a website that is perfect for your needs, it's only natural that you would want to find additional pages just like that one. Two features in Google's "Advanced Search" template—"Find Pages Similar to the Page" and "Find Pages That Link to the Page"—do exactly that. Once you've found a useful web page, find sites with similar content by popping the URL of that page into one of these search boxes. These search tools are not always 100 percent accurate, but the results are close enough for government work.

Cache

The web, you may have noticed, changes frequently. In its efforts to make sure that only the most recent information is made available, Google displays the information it has on hand from the last time it looked at a web page. But what if you wanted to see what a page looked like, not from Google's most recent effort but instead from the time before that? Google lets you peek at the state of a web page from its next-to-last look at a site.

To see what a web page looked like one session before the current one, click on the link labeled "cached" in the results list. It can be very informative when looking for material that has been removed from a website. That material is still retained and, therefore, retrievable in Google's cache. One reporter in Hawaii found this out when the journalist caught wind that a Hawaii state agency had inadvertently posted a confidential report from the Department of Homeland Security on the state's website. The report, detailing possible terror-attack scenarios, was supposed to be accessible only to state emergency-response officials. Still, the reporter Googled for the report. Like everyone else, he saw nothing but a 404 error message indicating a page that no longer existed. But by clicking on the *cached* link, the enterprising reporter found the report right there, hiding in plain sight, still alive in Google limbo.

Most web-savvy administrators now know that when they need to purge sensitive materials, they should ask Google to remove the questionable content, including the materials held in Google's pile of previous results waiting in the trash file for deletion.

Don't confuse Google's cached feature, which shows a snapshot from a prior visit, with a completely different service, unassociated with Google, known as the Wayback Machine. The Wayback Machine, a service of the Internet Archive, stores entire websites dating back to 1996 by periodically copying the sites whole. It is a great archival service that provides an easy way to see the web preserved in electronic amber. Pop in a URL and you can see websites as they were in days passed. If you have an itch to look at what a particular website looked like in 1999, the Wayback Machine will retro-rock you back to the days when InfoSeek was the dominant search engine and web searchers were fretting about the rules of Netiquette.

Reading Level

Beginner, intermediate, or advanced: you pick the sophistication level of the results of your search. This filter is handy for kids who may need the Dick-and-Jane version of specific subjects. Adults should stick to advanced, unless the topic is something dense like nuclear physics, epistemology, or the infield fly rule. Google designed the software by paying teachers to classify pages for different reading levels. The engineers then designed a statistical model that can compare a page with the model classification that the teachers designed to arrive at a reading-level rating. Google used the contents of Google Scholar to determine the level of language that would qualify as "advanced."

Language Tools

Google was born in the United States, but it's a citizen of the world. Perhaps owing to founder Sergey Brin's immigrant heritage—his parents are Russian, and Brin immigrated to the United States at the age of six—Google's language tools try to keep the world's linguistic barriers from interfering with the sharing of knowledge. On the Google home page, the link to "Language Tools" can be found by clicking the gear icon, they offer a handy way to quickly translate a word, phrase, or an entire website into English.

I'm not a linguist, but the international lawyers I know who use the translation tool all agree: the translations are . . . satisfactory. You will be able to get the gist of what was written in the foreign language, but the software still can come up with a howler every now and then. Some of the translations sound as if they were the handiwork of someone who got a C-plus in French class. The prose is clunky, but still, to see an entire text-dense web page of virtually any written tongue magically appear in (broken) English is a testament to Google's cleverness and its dedication to a world in which information is freed from restraints, including those of language.

Google Collections

Google is justifiably proud of its unique 80/20 workweek policy. Company professionals spend 80 percent of their time working on their usual projects and are not only permitted but encouraged to spend the other 20 percent of their time working on Google-related projects of personal interest. Google engineers have complained that that 80 percent is closer to 98 percent and that the 20 percent deep-think time doesn't always materialize. Nonetheless, this innovative flextime has resulted in some of Google's most interesting and useful new products since the introduction of the search engine. Grouped together, these products can be thought of as special data collections, arranged for easy retrieval by the same advanced search tools as the web but with the search focus trained on very specific types of information: news, alerts, books, finance, images, videos, and social media sites (such as blogs, online groups, and Google+).

Google News/Archives

If you haven't read the news today, go directly to Google News to see what you've been missing. With its search aimed directly at an estimated 20,000 news-only sites from around the globe, Google News makes the classic Associated Press news ticker, which spat out *rat-a-tat-tat* news around the clock last century, look like a clay tablet by comparison. Google News is fast, accurate, and constructed so that 1,200 versions of the same global story don't hog the front page. In fact, it is more akin to a customizable *USA Today*. Select a nation and Google News will happily fill in the top stories from there, along with relevant business, sports, and entertainment news.

If you haven't read the news today, go directly to Google News to see what you've been missing.

Google is hard at work on an archive of headlines and articles from more than 200 years of news. It will not be merely a tool to fetch the day's doings from a particular date but also a way to see the rise and fall of specific topics as part of an automatically generated timeline. Google is circumspect when it comes to talking about which newspapers will be included in the news archive, although the *New York Times* is an obvious choice. Solicitations for new content are prominent on the site as Google looks for additional content to beef up the collection.

Google Alerts

Searching news on the fly is great, but so is keeping track of it automatically. With Google Alerts, you'll be able to follow breaking news on your topics of interest from a variety of online sources: from the web in general or just from news sites, blogs, videos, or discussion groups. When setting up alerts, be sure to use the "Advanced Search" syntax and filter tools for targeted results. Stay current with developments in the news or on selected websites by storing your searches and asking for alerts when information changes. Google Alerts will email you when new results arrive on a web page or when a news story matching your query is posted to a recognized news site. Alert results can be emailed as they appear, once a day, or once a week—your choice.

Google Books

In 2004, armed with high-speed and accurate scanners equipped with optical character recognition (OCR) software, Google approached a number of institutional libraries with this proposition: If we show up at your library with our scanners, and if we pay for it, would you let us in to scan your millions of books in order to convert them into text-searchable pdf files?

Some of the most prestigious institutions in the world took Google up on its offer—Harvard University; Columbia University; the New York Public Library; Oxford University; and the state universities of California, Michigan, Texas, Virginia, and Wisconsin, among others— all agreed to let Google's scanners into the stacks.

Books that had been entombed on an obscure library shelf with very little hope of finding a reader now saw the light of day (if living on a server in a pdf document can rightly be called the light of day). In the earliest incarnation, the Google Books idea seemed like a dream come true for researchers: It promised to unearth otherwise inaccessible information. But fast-forward and you'll see that every-thing did not go smoothly in the Google Books project. A court settle-ment in 2009 established that copyright had been infringed upon, and Google could resume scanning only orphan works—books that are out of print or whose copyright protection has ended. It could also scan current books in print, but only snippets, and then only with the permission of the author or publisher. Still, that settlement did not completely resolve the legal issues affecting Google Books, and challenges in the court are still on the docket. In addition to copyright questions, other would-be electronic publishers and scholars are concerned about Google essentially owning a monopoly on the books of the past. The legal issues are complex but interesting. A blog for librarians titled *Google Book Settlement* keeps up with the ongoing litigation; I recommend it as a way of seeing how the law deals with the changes imposed by modern technology.

Whatever the results of the different lawsuits eventually turn out to be, Google's efforts to make a giant electronic library out of many print collections are impressive, and the value of Google Books to the researcher is undeniable. You could search the web all day and never put your finger on the exact quote you need from *Moby-Dick*. In the book version, it could take hours to thumb through the pages, past the descriptions of rendering blubber and a lunatic sea captain, to pin down the exact moment when Queequeg jumps into the sperm whale's head to rescue Tashtego. With a Google Books search, you can save the unfortunate fellow from the gunk in an instant.

The project is admirably ambitious. In its quest to digitize the world's books, the company first had to figure out just how many unique books exist. In a blog post, Google Books software engineer Leonid Taycher explained how they searched the global library systems, catalogs, and indices like the Library of Congress, WorldCat, and other comprehensive catalogs to come up with a number. Using complex algorithms and some commonsense filtering rules, Google determined that humans have produced 129,864,880 unique tomes. (Number subject to change.) It hasn't scanned them all yet, but digitizing the remaining titles is on Google's to-do list.

Books aren't the only things stored inside Google Books. Magazines are there too. Try pulling up some back copies of *New York* magazine from the 1970s to see why the hairstyles from the U.S. bicentennial year needed to go out of fashion. Use the "Advanced

Search" feature to locate books by any of the traditional means: title, author, publisher, date, subject, ISBN, and so on.

Google Finance

A mash-up of public information on public companies, Google Finance, an aggregation of corporate and financial information, pulls together real-time (or close to real-time) stock quotes, EDGAR filings, business news, blogs, chats, and analytical information all on a single page. For one-stop shopping for up-to-the-minute information on companies around the world, Google Finance is a tough act to beat. Use it to get a snapshot view of a public company and its current financial status. The chapter on company research will explain how to get a more detailed look at companies, but for quick reference, this service is excellent.

> **For one-stop shopping for up-to-the-minute information on companies around the world, Google Finance is a tough act to beat.**

Google Scholar

As the company describes the collection, Google Scholar contains "journal and conference papers, theses and dissertations, academic books, pre-prints, abstracts, technical reports, and other scholarly literature from all broad areas of research." For scholarly research, better resources are to be had at an academic library or from a large municipal library collection, but this site can be useful for retrieving cited material. Be cautious about depending on it for any in-depth research because there is no way to find out exactly what is contained in this database, and there is no guarantee that the materials are accurate. In my opinion, Google Scholar is a good idea that hasn't yet matured into a service that researchers can use reliably. The warning goes double for legal researchers. Even though Google Scholar contains decisions from the U.S. Supreme Court and state appellate courts, try Justia or one of the other free legal sites before you search Google Scholar. It's definitely not ready for prime-time legal research.

Other Google Tools

Social Tools

Although Facebook and Linkedin monopolize the headlines, Google also sponsors some very interesting social media tools. Old web hands who remember the Usenet groups from the 1990s-vintage Internet have found that social networking razzle-dazzle has not put the bulletin board services out to pasture. Google Groups, the successor to Usenet, is still zipping along, providing a meeting place for people with parochial interests. It's where you'll find very precisely defined bulletin board discussion groups where individuals can post and respond to questions that only twenty people in the world might care about. (And this to me has long been the Internet's grand gift—it combats isolation.) Google also makes it easy for anyone to become a blogger.

Google+ confronts Facebook's dominance in the social networking arena head-on. Not content to allow Facebook to monopolize the platform for I-had-tuna-fish-for-lunch threaded discussions, Google+ promises to give everyone's inner narcissist even more elbow room, allowing users to create social circles and post videos. Other than the fact that Google+ makes it easier to locate people, its value as a research tool doesn't look very promising.

iGoogle

I won't go into the details of iGoogle, since Google can describe its own services well enough. I'll just encourage you to set up a free iGoogle account as a way to homestead a little patch of cyberspace in the Cloud to call your own. Designed to compete with Microsoft, but especially to compete with Microsoft's world-standard Office Suite, iGoogle offers a free word processing program (Google has Docs, Microsoft has Word), spreadsheets (Google has Forms, Microsoft has Excel), calendar functionality (Google has Calendar, Microsoft has Outlook), email program (Google has Gmail, Microsoft has Outlook), RSS reader (Google has Google Reader, Microsoft has Internet Explorer) and the like. iGoogle makes a researcher's life easier by providing the same type of tools for free that otherwise would require an outlay of hundreds of dollars for the Microsoft equivalents. You'd be foolish to pass up one of the greatest deals on the web. The tools are powerful, and because the applications are all in the Cloud, your files are accessible from any web-connected spot on the planet.

The Rest of the Roster

Google eschews the snooze, constantly experimenting and devising new ways to understand the world by building better information tools. Web search, Google Maps, and Gmail are household names, but there are dozens of other Google services that serve online searchers, including online payment systems, shopping applications, health records services, and more. Since many of the services are helpful but don't have direct bearing on looking up information in the strictest sense, I'll just point you to Google's own "More Google Products" page, where you'll find capsule descriptions of the lesser-known tools. I recommend "Patent Search." I've filled up many idle hours rifling through applications looking for wacky, absurd, or undeservedly obscure inventions.

For additional information on the minutiae of Google searching, I recommend the site Google Guide for an exhaustive list of search operators. I've also found Search Engine Watch to be the most authoritative and timely site for keeping up with new Google services and developments. It is designed for webmasters who need to make sure that their own sites get proper visibility on Google, but the news, updates, and white papers that appear regularly are helpful to any researcher who's curious about the techniques of search to keep up with new developments.

SITES AND SOURCES MENTIONED IN THIS CHAPTER

"Books of the World, Stand Up and Be Counted! All 129,864,880 of You!"
http://booksearch.blogspot.com/2010/08/books-of-world-stand -up-and-be-counted.html

Facebook
www.facebook.com

Google Alerts
www.google.com/alerts

Google Books
http://books.google.com

Google Finance
http://finance.google.com

Google Groups
http://groups.google.com

Google Guide
www.googleguide.com

Google Language Tools
www.google.com/language_tools?hl=en

Google News
http://news.google.com

Google+
https://plus.google.com

Google Scholar
http://scholar.google.com

IANA Top-Level Domains
www.iana.org/domains/root/db

iGoogle
www.igoogle.com

Linkedin
www.linkedin.com

Search Engine Watch
http://searchenginewatch.com

Wayback Machine
www.archive.org/web/web.php

Why You Still Need a
Library Card

For information, for research, for learning, or for entertainment, there is no other institution quite as willing to share the wealth as a library. Whether we are talking about a few books on a shelf in a small school library or an immense research institution like the Library of Congress or the New York Public Library, where else can you get so much valuable stuff simply by asking for it? You don't need me to point out the obvious. Anytime you have a research question, one or more libraries should figure in the solution. Even with the Internet, a library and its resources still play a critical role in most research projects.

Even with the Internet, a library and its resources still play a critical role in most research projects.

My inclination was to start off a chapter describing libraries with some high-toned words from Shakespeare or Wordsworth or some other poetic heavyweight. Those plans were dashed when I serendipitously came across the ideal quote, courtesy of that late poet of late capitalism, Malcolm Forbes. Said the money-larded bard, "The richest person in the world—in fact all the riches in the world—couldn't provide you with anything like the endless, incredible loot available at your local library." The quote is not flowery, but then neither was Forbes. As a no-nonsense guy with an eye for a bargain, Malcolm was no sonneteer, but he gets the value of a library exactly right.

Right from the beginning, get rid of all the associations in your mind about libraries as dead dusty places staffed by those who delight in telling people to shut up. And stop thinking of a library as a place for dull, soul-draining work. Picture it instead as a place overflowing with limitless information that is there waiting for you to take whenever you need it. It's a place where you can find dedicated staff who have devoted their lives to mastering the techniques of research and who not only will help you but won't demand a fee for the assistance. Today's library is no longer some dingy backwater; it's a technologically advanced center for information retrieval, as up-to-date with online services as any place you've ever been. And while most libraries lack the coffee lounges of some bookstores, libraries don't get bent out of shape if you walk out the door with the goods without paying. Don't try getting away with that at your local bookstore. In short, libraries are better places than ever before to read and research.

Get to Know Your Library

Knowing how to work the library correctly is critical for those who want to find out anything, and things have changed since you first stepped into one in elementary school. One thing that hasn't changed, however, is that your first step is to equip yourself with a library card. By simply filling out a brief form and showing some ID, you stake your claim to an endless bounty. A library card gives you entrée into a club that is at once the most and least exclusive in the world. There are no velvet ropes to prevent anyone from joining the information giveaway party; libraries rightly pride themselves on being the most democratic institution imaginable. Public libraries are indeed public and will let anyone in the front door. What is exclusive about them is the grand collection of valuable goods gathered inside, available only to card-holders. Armed with a library card, any member can choose to do nothing with it or instead avail herself of all the services that most libraries provide. The choice of how little or how much value you derive from the library is yours. The library itself will be happy with whatever you decide. But get a library card. This is not negotiable. No researcher can survive long without one.

A library card gives you entrée into a club that is at once the most and least exclusive in the world.

The Catalog

Once you have yourself a library card, the next thing to do is find out what that card entitles you to. The library's catalog is your guide to everything. But before we get into the details, let us pause to remember the passing of every library lover's favorite feature, the card catalog. The digital age claimed the card catalog as one of its lamentable casualties. Long a standard feature in all libraries, the rows of wooden drawers filled with index cards is now as quaint as the eight-track player and the leisure suit. The card catalog was not only the best way to look up a library's holdings in the old days, it provided an undeniable tactile pleasure; flipping through the index cards made all that information concrete. The cards reliably did their prosaic job of pointing to books. Sometimes, patrons who came before you might have annotated the cards with advice on other sources to search and added recommendations that turned the otherwise plain bibliographic record into a miniature study guide. Even the catalog itself was lovely: those long oak drawers in a handsome cabinet were a grand piece of furniture; old library catalogs are in demand as antiques, as they are gradually retired from their service. Clearly, electronic catalogs are the new standard, and they have powers that the old system couldn't provide. Still, the old card catalog is sorely missed. But dry your tears, set the sentimentality aside, and forge ahead, because progress has its own comforts to offer.

The modern library catalog offers more than a road map to what a particular library holds. It can also provide links to useful websites. Often the catalog will tell you about books and materials held in associated libraries, so you are not limited to seeing only one library's collection. It is fast and accurate, and, thanks to the modern miracle of hyperlinking, cross-referencing interesting information doesn't take all day.

All catalogs index the collection by the eternal triumvirate of search possibilities: *author, title, subject*. These search fields haven't gone away, but they are not the only way to search. E-catalogs open the door to far more elaborate and far more precise searching. The reason for that is the widespread adoption of an electronic system for cataloging that makes each individual bibliographic record a marvel of concise detail.

The bibliographic record, which is the professionally crafted description of an item, is a minor literary exercise in itself. The record provides the author, title, and subject information that you would expect, but it also delivers a deftly written description of an item's physical dimensions, its call number, its International Standard Book Number (ISBN), its Library of Congress Control Number (LCCN), identifiers (unique numbers that identify a specific work), hyperlinks to other resources (when relevant), and many other technical details. Needless to say, the catalog also describes non-book holdings. Significant parts of most library collections are periodicals, such as magazines, journals, and newspapers; database services, like ProQuest and EBSCO; and subscription websites. Catalogs account for these types of sources and make them findable too.

Today, the most widely used standard for cataloging books is the MARC record. Librarians use the MARC (Machine-Readable Cataloging) system and its fill-in-the-blank form as a way to make sure that the description of the items in the collection follow certain rules. This approach leads to consistency in the records and results in a dependable system that readers can use to search holdings quickly. Librarians like the system because a single title, which might be held by thousands of different libraries, can be cataloged by one person or the publisher but can be used by all libraries that contain that item in their collection.

The elegance of the MARC record is that if one computer can read the data, other computers can too. For all the charm of the idiosyncratic cards in the card catalog, MARC records take much of the guesswork out of cataloging a book or other item, so that descriptions are predictable. The net effect is that you, the reader in search of a book, have a reliable method of finding that book in any number of sources. The town library of Ballplay, Alabama, catalogs its books exactly the same way as does the Library of Congress. The process is less quaint than the old days, and it's plenty faster and more accurate to boot.

I introduce the MARC system as a way to show you how to mine the details of a book's record to help you better find your way through a library catalog. Locate an item of interest—the kind of title that makes you say, "Oh, yeah, that's *exactly* what I am looking for"—and the bibliographic record will help you find additional titles from that book's extended family. You could search for similar items by author to find other titles by the same person or by keyword to see what other works fall within the same category. You can also quickly search for a specific holding by using a book's unique identifier: its LCCN or ISBN; for a periodical, use its International Standard Serial Number (ISSN). Depending on the catalog, you can create very precise searches by mixing and matching search terms for things like names, electronic titles, publication information, series information (for periodicals), and the identifying numbers.

The beauty of the catalog is that you can look over the entire library landscape in one place, quickly mastering a vast domain with some very simple searches. A well-designed catalog will help you locate what you need with a minimum of fuss. It also will help you request the materials you've found, point you to additional materials of interest, and save you many hours of fruitless Internet searching.

> **The beauty of the catalog is that you can look over the entire library landscape in one place, quickly mastering a vast domain with some very simple searches.**

If you want to try something interesting, cruise around the catalogs of libraries located worldwide by connecting via Libdex to any of the 17,000+ libraries who allow visitors. If you're looking for a book to tell you everything you need to know about Tasmanian devils, chances are good that a library in Auckland will be able to suggest a title or two. You may not be able to put your hands on the book itself, but knowing that a title exists provides the information you'll need to find it in a local research library or by interlibrary loan.

And as much as it pains me not to be able to recommend the library for everything, both Amazon.com and Barnes & Noble have very powerful book catalog software that any first-rate library would envy.

Special Services

Libraries, contrary to appearance, are not book warehouses. Row upon row of books just sitting there on the shelf may look like a still life, but libraries are, in fact, surprisingly lively places with a great deal of work going on behind the scenes and in the stacks themselves. And librarians do much more than dust the books and make sure that they are put back on the shelves in the right order. Most libraries make available a wide range of services designed to boost your research. The breadth of these special services depends on the size and budget of your local institution, but these services are generally available from most municipal libraries. It is very much worth your while to check in with your local branch to see what they have on the menu.

Most libraries make available a wide range of services designed to boost your research.

Articles and Databases

Part of any researcher's due diligence is seeing what has been written in the press. Google News is a fair way to look through newspapers, but you will serve yourself better by using a commercial service designed specifically as a searchable archive of newspaper and magazine articles. Individuals who have access to a Nexis account are fortunate. It is the gold standard for searching newspapers, magazines, newsletters, and news wires for articles and news stories, but it does not come cheap. Nexis does sell limited access to individuals, but it prefers to sell access to companies and institutions rather than to a single person. The next best thing is access to articles databases, and this is where a library card comes in handy.

Many libraries will provide their cardholders with access to services that allow you search articles for free. Exactly what services are available vary from library to library—the New York Public Library lists more than 600 electronic indices, but you should check your library's website or ask the staff about which databases are available. Depending on the service, the library will give access to their cardholders; in other instances, the library subscribes to the service but limits access to the library staff. In either event, you should certainly keep your eyes peeled for these standard databases. Most libraries have them, and they can do the heavy lifting for research into current and historical information.

- **America's Historical Newspapers (1690–1922):** A searchable electronic version of old newspapers that once were archived in microfilm, microfiche, or as a yellowing pile of newsprint on some library shelf just waiting for the right moment to burst into flames. This archive is easy to use and less likely to combust.

- **Credo Reference:** A one-stop reference service that pulls information from encyclopedias, dictionaries, biographies, and other works with a single search.

- **EBSCO Research Database:** A database containing the searchable full texts of newspapers and magazines.

- **ProQuest:** A commercial database that serves up doctoral dissertations, academic journals, and genealogy information as well as abstracts for the natural sciences, social sciences, arts and humanities, and technology.

The mother of all databases is Dialog, now owned by ProQuest. It began life in 1964, in the early days of the Space Age, as a way to help engineers from what was then the Lockheed Missile and Space Company find science and engineering articles and help them navigate the company's immense data files. For librarians of a certain age, Dialog was the first electronic database they learned. It predated all the now-standard online services like Nexis, Factiva, and Westlaw and was a standard tool long before the web was invented. Mastering the arcane Boolean logic and commands needed to retrieve data from the service felt like learning some occult language from the Middle Ages. Today, Dialog is still a large-scale research service that comprises hundreds of individual files collectively containing more than 2 billion individual records. The records in each file are abstracts or full-text articles from many academic disciplines. Exactly what Dialog contains is too detailed to list here, but the complete rundown of the files and what each contains is online in the "Dialog Bluesheets." The name is a holdover from the print days, when descriptions of what was in each file and the methods for searching were printed on, well, blue sheets of paper. (Giving things clever names was not Lockheed's core competency.) To this day, Dialog is still a powerful search tool. Access is usually restricted to the library staff, but they can search on behalf of patrons.

Digital Materials and Special Collections

Libraries are not just about books any more. One of the great things about the digital age is how much can be easily digitized. Google Books, of course, is working on the books and will continue to do so, depending on how the lawsuits progress. More to the point, every publisher is tossing and turning at night figuring out how to get his e-books onto every computer tablet and e-reader around the world. Gutenberg had moveable type; today, it's portable type.

Thanks to the wonders of digitization, libraries not only catalog items but can also deliver e-files to users anywhere in the world. The Prints and Photographs Divisions of the Library of Congress, for example, makes available more than half of its million items in downloadable format. (They also will scan previously unscanned materials from the collection on demand for a small fee, download the high-resolution file onto a CD, and mail it to patrons.)

In digital format, this immense repository of Americana can offer the researcher immediate access to a remarkable array of historic materials. Not to be outdone, most library systems in the United States offer patrons thousands of downloadable e-books, audiobooks, and videos. And when you can play *The Best of Snoop Dogg* on your home computer courtesy of your local library, you understand that libraries are no longer the starchy old tombs of popular imagination. Many libraries even offer Freegal, a service that allows patrons to help themselves to three free songs each week from Sony Music.

Manuscripts and Historical Archives

In addition to providing access to current information, a library also serves as an archive. You should be able to locate repositories of original documents and historical artifacts like maps, diaries, deposited collections of papers, and other materials held at libraries throughout the country. Biographers would have no source material if a library did not accept the accumulated letters and papers of accomplished individuals. Historians rely on humble materials like diaries, commercial records from ordinary businesses, and collections of personal papers to reconstruct daily life from years gone by. And newspaper archives, the so-called first draft of history, can contain clues to people, places, and things that might otherwise be forgotten. In this way, a library preserves the past and makes it accessible to the present.

> **In addition to providing access to current information, a library also serves as an archive.**

Basic Services

Borrowing Privileges

The very essence of a library, especially the public library, can be found in its policy of lending books and other materials to its cardholders. This is what makes a library one of the greatest democratic institutions in the world: You only have to ask, and the library will give. If there is a better social idea than providing citizens with unrestricted access to the recorded knowledge of the world, I have yet to hear it.

Computers

When the Internet was still a novelty, libraries across the country were gearing up for it, and by 2005, according to the American Library Association, almost 99 percent of public libraries offered free access to computers and the Internet. Providing the public with computers is still a basic service from all libraries. You can always count on finding a computer in a public library when you need one.

Interlibrary Loan

Many libraries can borrow materials from other area libraries. That way, a smaller library can serve as a branch of a larger one. If your local branch doesn't keep a particular book in its collection, you can request it from another library that does.

Holds

When you are really in a fever to read a book, it's aggravating to discover that every time you try to borrow it, it is still off the shelf. You can take a measure of revenge against the slow readers in your neighborhood, who take out books and then keep renewing them, by placing a hold on the book. The library then will not allow the person who currently has the book checked out to extend his or her sign-out period.

Reserves

At college and university libraries, professors may place certain materials in reserve for the classes they teach. Reserves usually have a brief circulation time, if they circulate at all, so that students have a reasonable chance of accessing materials in a timely manner.

Reference Services

So far, we mostly have discussed how to find out information on your own. From time to time, even the best researcher gets stumped and needs some assistance. When you are facing down a brick wall and not finding what you need, call in the professionals. Reference librarians are every researcher's secret weapon. The men and women who staff the reference desk aren't there just to give directions to the rest room. They are skilled in the craft of finding information and bring a professional's experience and judgment to the task. Asking a question of a reference librarian is not bothering them; far from it. There's nothing that a self-respecting librarian likes better than a challenging question. To them, research is not a task, it's a calling, and the satisfaction of locating an answer to a difficult question is the most rewarding part of the profession. So don't ever be shy. Got a question you can't quite answer? They'll be glad to help you.

> Reference librarians are every
> researcher's secret weapon.

Recommendations and Guides

Librarians understand how daunting it is to search through a catalog of millions of items. To simplify the process for their patrons, they often write guides to specific types of information, describing where and how to find materials on a selected subject. These guides are known as *pathfinders*. A good pathfinder in the library can be a

WHAT DO REFERENCE LIBRARIANS DO?

Before you can get a reference librarian working on your research, you, of course, must first get in touch with one. Contacting a librarian these days could not be any easier. The simplest way to ask a librarian a question is to go to the library and ask in person, but they can also be reached via email, chat, or phone. Check your local library's website for an "Ask a Librarian" link. No matter how you contact the library, staff will be happy to take your request. There is no guaranteed turnaround time for most requests, but research librarians usually will set right to work on your question.

A librarian offers more than a free set of hands; you're getting the services of a skilled professional. You also are taking advantage of the librarian's access to many more resources than you probably have on your own. Chances are good too that the reference librarian will quickly know how to approach a research question effectively. You will be talking to someone who knows where to look for information. Really good research librarians make research look like miracle work; years of experience and mastery of the sources gives them insight that most casual researchers won't enjoy. In short, make the librarian your ally and partner in research. Best of all, with the exception of certain premium services, all this know-how and far-ranging access to resources is free.

lifesaver—it will cut right to the chase. Such guides encapsulate the librarian's hard-earned expertise in a simple, digestible format. Ask for them by name (as in, "Do you have a pathfinder on meteorology?").

Premium Services

If you have a budget or work for a company that can spend some money for research, you can take advantage of the premium services of a large library. In this way, smaller companies that cannot afford to keep a librarian on staff can still essentially hire a library staff and access a vast collection without the expense of actually operating a library. The following are some of the fee-based premium services offered from the Library of Congress and the New York Public Library (NYPL); check with your local system to see what's available to you:

- **Reproductions for editorial or commercial use:** Some libraries have access to photos, artwork, and other graphic materials that can be used in patrons' commercial publications.

- **Document delivery:** The NYPL can photocopy or electronically scan books, newspapers, documents, and other items for delivery by email in pdf format. Not only can librarians mine the riches of their own huge collections but they have access to other suppliers, allowing them to "obtain virtually any document," as the NYPL promises.

- **Digital imaging:** The Prints and Photographs Division of the Library of Congress has one of the coolest services in the bibliosphere: on-demand imaging. Should you need to get your hands on a high resolution copy of a Mathew Brady photograph of Abraham Lincoln or a map from 1908 or any of the other half million scanned-in items from the library's extensive collection, they will oblige.

Special Collection Libraries

For more in-depth research, especially when
looking in great detail for a specific subject,
it is helpful to rely on the services of a
special-interest library.

The municipal library is probably the most familiar type of library to the casual researcher. But for more in-depth research, especially when looking in great detail for a specific subject, it is helpful to rely on the services of a special-interest library. Special collections tend to have more generous selections of a limited subject matter, and the staff can provide more expertise in that area than a generalist in a less focused institution.

As the term implies, special libraries exist that either restrict the type of information they hold to a specific subject or are attached to another institution, such as a museum or academy. In fact, larger museums, halls of fame, and professional associations almost always maintain a library for use by their members or patrons. In many cases, curators will happily field questions from the general public.

When you need to have an obscure fact checked, these specialty libraries are a godsend. Some years ago, a friend of mine who is an avid collector of the works of Irish playwright Samuel Beckett heard that Beckett, while on a visit to New York in 1964, attended a New York Mets double-header. He asked me to track down the box score for the games. Two phone calls later, the researchers from the library at the National Baseball Hall of Fame in Cooperstown, New York, had the answer. And while helping research a lawsuit involving Seneca Nation of Indians land claims against the state of New York, the librarians from the

Museum of the American Indian (in the Bronx, no less) were an invaluable help. They provided collected works from the 1800s, including original treaties and scholarly studies of how the Seneca Nation operated at the time the original land deeds and leases were signed, much of which went into the legal papers and exhibits submitted to court.

THE CHANGING LIBRARY

The traditional library, for hundreds of years known fundamentally as a collection of cataloged books, is changing drastically. As a society, we are reimagining how we store knowledge and distribute it. The epochal shift from print to the web and from the idea that information is stored "just in case" to a world in which we can put our hands on the things we need to know "just in time" is a profound change that has happened over the past thirty years. As technology drives these changes, amendments to the law will also remake the way most researchers go about their business.

The utopian idea of a knowledge commons turns on the idea that knowledge is a necessity and ought not be owned, like air and water. Rather than adhere to the traditional idea of ownership of information through copyright protections, information producers instead seek to make their learning widely available at little or no cost. Exactly how scholarship and research will be shared in a world that still jealously guards information remains to be seen, but the idea is already under discussion at a number of universities. Libraries will be players in this new world by helping connect researchers to the resources or through facilitating the storage and dissemination of this brave new world of information.

Name your field of interest and chances are good a special library exists that contains both a useful collection and a knowledgeable staff to help you find very specific information not otherwise available online or at a general interest library. A good way to find out about special collections is to check a directory of archives. Most large libraries subscribe to ArchiveGrid, ArchivesUSA, or Archive Finder, which can point you to 5,000 repositories of archival information in the United States, the United Kingdom, and Ireland.

Public Library of Science

A perfect example of the new era in information access is the Public Library of Science (PLoS). This noble nonprofit effort aims to make

---

TRY THIS AT HOME

• Use Libdex to find out if any libraries in Zimbabwe have books on French architecture. Do libraries in China have anything on pangolins?

• Find a library that collects cookbooks and recipes. (Note: There are a number of them.)

• Identify libraries that hold doctoral dissertations, with an emphasis on the social sciences.

• Contact your local library and find out what special reference services are offered by asking one of the reference librarians. While you are talking to the researcher, get a name and an email address so that you always have a research contact at your disposal.

"the world's scientific and medical literature a freely available public resource." To do that the organization enlists researchers to make their papers accessible without restriction. Subscribers pay a small fee to PLoS to help finance the operation, but any subsequent use is free to any other user who wants to look at or cite the research.

This effort is the practical result of the initial Internet *cri de coeur* that "information wants to be free." What started with a few dedicated graduate students typing book texts into an antique computer has now become an international effort to make human learning not the exclusive property of the elite but the birthright of all literate citizens.

Other Special-Interest Libraries

The following list of twelve special-interest libraries will give you a taste of the types available. The predominance of branches of my hometown New York Public Library in this list is not an act of urban chauvinism but is instead a reflection of the long years of civic support New York City and its diverse citizens have provided for such specialized libraries. Check your nearest big-city system for any special collections it might hold or have access to.

Arthur Lakes Library—Colorado School of Mines
http://library.mines.edu

EEA Library—AirVenture Museum
http://museum.eaa.org/collection/library.asp

June F. Mohler Fashion Library—Kent State University
www.library.kent.edu/page/10507

Cine Deloria Jr. Library—National Museum of the American Indian
www.sil.si.edu/libraries/nmai

New York Public Library for the Performing Arts, Dorothy and Lewis B. Cullman Center
www.nypl.org/locations/lpa

Rock and Roll Hall of Fame Museum Library and Archives
http://rockhall.com/library/resources

Schomburg Center for Research in Black Culture—New York Public Library
www.nypl.org/locations/schomburg

Science, Industry and Business Library—New York Public Library
www.nypl.org/locations/sibl

U.S. Military Academy Cadet Library at West Point
http://usmalibrary.usma.edu

SITES AND SOURCES MENTIONED IN THIS CHAPTER

Archive Finder
http://archives.chadwyck.com

ArchiveGrid
http://archivegrid.org

"The History of Dialog"
www.dialog.com/about/history/transcript.shtml

Libdex
www.libdex.com

Library of Congress

www.loc.gov

Prints and Photographs Division of the Library of Congress

www.loc.gov/pictures

New York Public Library

www.nypl.org

ProQuest

www.proquest.com/en-US

Public Library of Science

www.plos.org

A Reference Desk to Call Your Own

You may never have noticed this, but one thing is a constant in library design the world over: The shelves closest to the librarians' desks are where they keep the reference books. It's no coincidence, and there is no mystery about why reference books are stored up close. These are the sources librarians use most, and to save themselves long treks into the spider-filled recesses at the back of the stacks, they wisely keep them close at hand.

Reference resources are tomes or databases in which facts are gathered so that readers can look up information quickly; they are, by definition, authoritative, timely, and credible. For anyone who aspires to learn how to find out anything, cultivating an appreciation for the value of good reference materials is a must. Go-to reference works like dictionaries, encyclopedias, and atlases are trustworthy stockpiles of facts. These compendiums of useful data should be the constant companions of any researcher, student, reporter, writer, or information junkie. The best advice I can give you is to take a cue from sensible librarians everywhere and fashion a reference collection of your own.

The best advice I can give you is to take a cue from sensible librarians everywhere and fashion a reference collection of your own.

Libraries commit a substantial chunk of their budget to keeping those print volumes standing at attention at the reference desk for quick consultation. You can get yours mostly for free. At that price, there is no reason not to equip yourself with an extensive personal library. In just about every project, you'll use reference titles constantly. Have them at your fingertips so that you can quickly find some pesky fact or verify a simple date. Because we are talking mostly about the online world here, a DIY reference library requires little more than a clear idea of what type of information you need to look up frequently, some time to track down resources that deliver the goods when you need to answer a question, and insatiable curiosity.

The easier it is to consult these sources, the better, so spend some time thinking about how to organize them in your browser's "Favorites" or "Bookmarks" and then start loading in the URLs. Everyone's list will be different, but at a minimum your reference library should contain:

- A dictionary and thesaurus

- An almanac

- A basic encyclopedia

- An atlas

- A directory of products and manufacturers

- Tables for equations, mathematics, and conversions

- A collection of quotations

- A basic history of the United States and the world

- A library catalog

- A searchable collection of classic literature

To help you stock your personal reference shelf, I recommend a source for each one these items, almost all of them free. After jump-starting your collection, we'll look at some superb reference portals. These are sites stocked with thousands of links to fact-filled sites. These compilations of reference sites are terrific, and I cannot recommend them enough. We'll wrap up the chapter by taking a look at how you can search out reference sources specific to your own research needs. In the meantime, let's start with the basics.

Basic References

Dictionary

Topping every list of vital reference resources is a good online dictionary. I'm a big fan of YourDictionary.com. The site delivers not only a first-rate dictionary, with the expected definitions, etymologies, and links to synonyms but also a thesaurus and links to specialty dictionaries. It has glossaries to explain the opaque jargon from the worlds of finance and computer science as well as scientific and medical definitions. Best of all, YourDictionary.com solves that age-old grammar school head-scratcher: How do you look up the correct spelling of a word in the dictionary when you don't know how to spell the word in the first place? Try wild card searching. (Is it "accommodate" or "accomodate"? Look it up by typing "acco**odate" to find out.) Spelling is not the only web-enhanced feature either. Click on the "Hear It" link to listen to a disembodied voice with perfect diction pronounce the defined word, relieving you of the burden of trying to puzzle out what all those arcane pronunciation symbols mean. (It's *RIB-ald*, not *RYE-bald*.)

In the twenty-first-century world of texting shorthand, the acronym and abbreviation finder (click "Other Dictionaries") will help you make sense of what your teenagers are saying as they wear their thumbs raw sending messages to their friends. "Other Dictionaries" also leads to an eclectic array of specialty dictionaries, covering topics such as idioms, golf, robotics, leather, and labor relations. And for the diligent writer who's determined not to let a participle dangle or an infinitive split, dozens of articles on English grammar and usage will guide you effortlessly through the exciting world of expository writing. When it comes to language and word information, Your Dictionary.com is the best on the web. A Swiss Army knife for all things linguistic, this site is like having an entire wall full of books at the end of a hyperlink.

Almanac

With a great dictionary now stowed in your personal reference collection, add an almanac, a glorious reference tool that's indispensable for quick access to facts, figures, and obscure data. For most professional researchers, *The World Almanac* is the source for the course.

This hefty collection of factual information gathered in one place can save hours of online searching. (I can't repeat it enough times: Don't go hunting for information yourself if someone has already found it for you!) You'll find summaries of world news, biographies, arts and entertainment, and health and science to name a few. This one, however, is not an online giveaway. You'll need to buy a print copy, but at less than $20, it's a worthwhile purchase. If you're in a book-buying mood, it wouldn't hurt to spring for the *Information Please Almanac* to supplement the *World Almanac*. It's filled with current facts and more U.S. materials than the world version.

Atlas

In days past, no self-respecting library would open its door if it didn't have a good, up-to-date atlas. Atlases are still important, but the days are over when an oversize book with maps of the nations of the world is the best way to find out where the cities of France are located. Now, of course, we have Google Maps, which serves simultaneously as an atlas, a road map, and tour guide. It features scaleable maps, driving or walking directions from virtually any point on earth to another one on the same contiguous land mass, and satellite pictures mixed in with street-level photographs. It's a virtuoso performance of information organization and display. Download Google Earth, and you've got yourself a set of Cartier-level cartography that would have driven Magellan mad with envy.

The two Google geography products should serve to answer most basic questions, but the ambitious researcher might supplement the Google Maps and Google Earth collection with a number of other excellent geographic tools. Two resources for looking up place names in the United States are the USGS Geographic Names Information

Service, with almost two million standardized names of places and geographic features, and the U.S. Census Bureau's U.S. Gazetteer. And for anything else map related, the Arizona State University library has a terrific collection of geographic reference materials that should serve your world exploration needs perfectly. Remember too that specially designed atlases can indicate everything from the distribution of mineral deposits to agricultural growing regions. Check the Arizona State library site for pointers on using these single-purpose maps.

Demographic Information

Demographic information is always in demand, especially for business researchers. Say you have an idea to open a restaurant that would cater to families with young children. You'd want to know where you would find communities with a significant population of people with young children. To generate a demographic profile of towns, cities, and counties around the nation, use the U.S. Census Bureau's American FactFinder. FactFinder takes the raw data collected from the decennial census and digests it into comprehensible reports and charts. For business and marketing purposes, the demographic data giveaway is a boon to researchers. But it's not business researchers alone who can profit from FactFinder's geographic, economic, and housing data. For the big statistical picture of the United States, this site deserves a special place in your reference toolkit. There invariably will come a time when you will need to get a sense of fundamental information about the population in the United States, such as average age or ethnic characteristics. A company planning to sell shoe styles that appeal to women aged thirty-five to fifty-five would be remiss in not checking on exactly how many potential customers live in a given city. FactFinder specializes in this type of information. Speaking of the Census Bureau, it once published the annual *Statistical Abstract: The National Data Book*, a collection of the charts and graphs from all the major government agencies. The book, alas, fell victim to budget cutting. The abstracts were a statistical digest to all the things that the federal government measures. Older editions can still serve as a guide to the many thousands of statistic reports from all over Uncle Sam's bureaucratic estate.

To generate a demographic profile of towns, cities, and counties around the nation, use the U.S. Census Bureau's American FactFinder.

Encyclopaedia Britannica

So why can't you just bookmark Wikipedia and be done with it? Because you're smarter than that is why. While millions of misguided users obliviously feast on the easy-to-use Wikipedia entries, they do so in defiance of the site's egregious shortcomings. These drawbacks invalidate it as a reliable source for a conscientious researcher. After all, the information is written by editors who in many instances have no professional credentials. In addition, the site is updated only when someone feels like it, and bias can easily enter into its seemingly impartial profiles of a subject. Better to bypass the easy, but suspect, pickings of Wikipedia and head instead to a long-trusted source with a history of accuracy and sober scholarship, the *Encyclopaedia Britannica* (EB). For concise explanations of complex subjects, encyclopedias are terrific. Frequently, an encyclopedia can jump-start your research by providing a nutshell view of the topic in question. Search for "mercury" and see two- and three-paragraph write-ups on the planet, the NASA program, the chemical, the Roman god, and the plant.

To Wikipedia's credit, it outshines the donnish worthies when it comes to pop culture, passing fads, and ephemera. Its entry for "mercury" includes exhaustive references to, among many things, the car brand, the record label, antique airplanes, the lead singer from Queen, naval vessels, hockey teams, and H. L. Mencken's magazine, all of which are MIA from the more high-toned encyclopedia.

The EB comes in two flavors, free and premium. The free service isn't shabby, but the premium service, at just north of $100 a year for a subscription, is a bargain like you never saw. The EB drafts scholars, scientists, university professors, and others with totally ripped brains to write the articles. Right from the start, EB authors have more credibility than the average Wikipedia editor, whose CV may consist of little more than a browser and an afternoon to kill by typing up deep thoughts about Steely Dan.

Library Catalog

Don't yawn just yet, because I am about to explain how a good library catalog is a near-perfect tool for finding experts. In any event, you are going to need access to a proper catalog to see what's been written on the subject you are researching. No matter if you are browsing through the catalog of a small town library or the Library of Congress,

> **A good library catalog is a near-perfect tool for finding experts.**

the fundamental purpose of a catalog is to let you know what the library holds, searchable by the ever-eternal triumvirate of author, subject, and title. Today's electronic catalogs are masterful indices that can deliver more information than you could possibly want on each item in the collection. So, by all means, use the library catalog for its original purpose: to find out if the library has a book on what you need to find.

The web has opened the door to using the average catalog in an entirely new way. It's a database of experts. This makes perfect sense when you remember the cliché we use to indicate that someone knows a lot about something: "Oh, he wrote the book on it!" As with most clichés, there is a germ of truth in this one. If we buy the premise that an author is, by definition, an expert in his or her subject, it follows that the Library of Congress catalog is not only a list of everything that the library owns but is also a free guide that names the names of millions of people, dead or alive, who are experts in their fields. We will be liberal with the definition of *expert*, because not every book is a masterpiece, but the library catalog will quickly tell you who cares enough about a subject to write a book about it.

Say you need to locate an expert on some very specialized subject, like the history of geodesic domes or the mating habits of electric eels or how children acquire language skills. You could succumb to your natural urge to use Google as a way to find this presumed-to-exist expert—and if so, good luck to you. Or you could save yourself an aspirin-bottle's worth of headache by first finding out who has written books about your subject. Once you've gotten an idea of who the relevant authors are, you're halfway to having a quotable expert in your pocket. Authorship is like a union card for subject experts.

When you start your catalog browsing, set aside plenty of time for the task. You'll be amazed at the breadth of information waiting for you, so don't rush your research. I recommend the catalog from the

Library of Congress for your first stop because it is the largest and most inclusive catalog in the world. The New York Public's catalog is not exactly small potatoes either.

When searching, really turn your subject over thoroughly. What you want to do is identify (1) some books you might want to read and (2) the names of some authors you might want to contact for follow up questions. (*Hint*: Living authors are more helpful than dead ones, if only because they have email.) Search using synonyms, and click on an author's name to find out what other books he has written. Think of your catalog searching time as a leisurely stroll through a particularly fascinating theme park. Take your time, and use your imagination. The library catalog, when used imaginatively, will no longer be merely a pedestrian search tool, but an invaluable aid for identifying experts. Looking through the catalog is better than Googling for an expert because you won't have to slog through blog posts, news stories, and other distractions. The catalog is professionally edited, concise, and accurate. The information about these author-experts will be of much better quality than what you could find with a Google search alone.

Once you've diligently searched and come up with a list of titles and authors in whom you may be interested, the next step in the process of finding experts is to read the relevant books and, if you still have questions, to get in touch with the author. For contacting authors, my advice is twofold: search online to see if you can find an email address (see Chapter 7) or website for the author; if that doesn't pan out, get in touch with the book publisher and ask them to forward your questions to the author. Except for some celebrated eccentrics like the late J. D. Salinger or Salman Rushdie, most writers would be thrilled to hear from their readers. Academic authors can usually be reached at their schools, institutional authors at their businesses, and modern ones through their websites. This is one of those cases where using a database like a library catalog in conjunction with Google is a beautiful and elegant way to find very specific information that you could not unearth by conducting an Internet search alone.

Products and Manufacturers

Although digital products are the current darlings of the economy, things fashioned from extruded plastic, bent metal, and sawn wood are still a very important part of the manufacturing world. If you need to contact a company that makes some quotidian product like zippers, then ThomasNet is where you'll find the info. This unprepossessing site holds a masterfully designed database of company information that can provide the answer to questions like "Who makes left-handed scissors?" (Walter Stern Inc. of Port Washington, New York, for one) and "What company manufactures piano benches?" (the Georgia Chair Company, among others, is who). ThomasNet got its start as a multivolume set of books known as the *Thomas Register*, remarkable not only for the breadth of its directory coverage for manufacturers, but also for the books' brilliant Kelly green covers. Even when you don't have specific question in mind, it's fun to browse the site just to see the range of very weird objects for sale. After all, *someone* has to make "getter pumps to pass current directly through titanium alloy in a vacuum to sublimate it." ULVAC Technologies Inc., we salute you.

Quotations

A pithy quote, an epigram, or a joke can sometimes sum up exactly what you need to say in a report, a speech, or a presentation. The collected wisdom of great writers who can express in five words what it takes the rest of us fifty to say is a very useful thing to have at your disposal. The Quotations Page will serve a modern audience well. (Also see Bartleby.com, discussed later in this chapter.)

Searchable Collection of Classic Literature

Although I sincerely wanted to keep this list of essential reference resources restricted to the best of breed, there were too many good selections to pick from, and, really, there is no good reason to be stingy with the picks. There are three worthy candidates for this category, all free, and all deserving of a place in your reference collection.

Project Gutenberg

Before there were Kindles, before there was Amazon.com, and before there were iPads, there was Project Gutenberg. Founder Michael Hart set about creating e-texts in the 1970s, long before the advent of the web and public access to the Internet. Today, more than 33,000 plain-text versions of books new and old are downloadable from the Gutenberg site, all of them free. The texts are fully functional but nothing fancy. Hart himself minces no words when he says his goal was to produce works that the average reader could enjoy. His goal was not to provide a perfect specimen of a book text that would pass muster with a scholar but rather a serviceable e-version of classic works. In that he has succeeded, and that makes this a keeper for your electronic reference shelf.

Bartleby.com

Another major reference source for classic literature and poetry is Bartleby.com, named for Herman Melville's recalcitrant law copyist. Formerly known as the Bartleby Project, this collection of classics was one of the earliest web projects to turn books into electronically searchable and readable formats on a large scale. Founder and CEO Steven H. van Leeuwen started the site in 1993 with a single electronic title, Walt Whitman's *Leaves of Grass*. Today, you have at your fingertips some of the great works of Western literature and scholarship, including Shakespeare, the King James Bible, *Bartlett's Familiar Quotations*, and the *Cambridge History of English and American Literature*.

Google Books

Where there's smart, there's Google. Yet again it earns itself a place in our galaxy of reference stars, this time for Google Books. We looked at the service in some detail in Chapter 3, and it deserves a place in this chapter as well.

Tables of Math Equations

An old joke holds there are three types of people in the world: those who can count and those who can't. As someone squarely in the latter group, the idea of performing arithmetic much more challenging than dividing twenty-five by five gives me hives. Luckily, there's Math.com. Although it is designed for young students, with its helpful collection of calculators, converters, formulas, and tables, it's also great for numerically challenged researchers.

And there you have it. You may not realize it now, but you have just put together a reference library that will grant you access to literally thousands of books and millions of facts and will equip you to search for an immense variety of information at little or no cost and with very little effort. These greatest hits represent only a core collection.

Reference Portals

To really flesh out your research, you'll need to customize your reference library with links to sources of specific interest to the subjects you need to reference most. Let's take a look at some must-see collections. Feel free to review the list and pluck out the items that you think will be most helpful to you and just keep them handy to consult.

You'll need to customize your reference library with links to sources of specific interest to the subjects you need to reference most.

RefDesk

At the top of the list is the aptly named RefDesk.com. Calling itself the "Fact Checker for the Internet," RefDesk.com is a grand bazaar of facts and sources, exhaustive and eclectic. The first thing you'll notice is that the site looks as if it were designed by someone with better things to do than prettify a website. But what the site lacks in glitz, it more than compensates for with a jaw-dropping collection of links to an immense variety of sources. Scroll down through the amusing collection of daily updates, and you will come upon one of the most marvelous collections of reference sources ever amassed in one place.

Need to find a database to look up toll-free numbers? It's here. Want to verify that the knee bone's connected to the shinbone? Check *Gray's Anatomy*. Can a committee chairman second a motion? Check *Robert's Rules of Order*. We could go on in this vein all week. Symptoms of beriberi? Grover Cleveland's religion? The name and title of the head of state for Zimbabwe? How much is a 2002 Dodge Stratus worth? These are all findable facts from one or several of the links on RefDesk.com. Spend an afternoon simply browsing through the collection to see what links you might want to appropriate for your own use. The site is a doozy; I promise that you'll find something of interest here. It trumps Google as a source for facts because the founder, Dr. Bob Drudge, has done his homework. The sites he selects for his search categories are excellent deep web databases. Why monkey around with trying to locate what day of the week April 19, 2053, falls on in Google when RefDesk.com can connect you to a perpetual calendar?

Virtual Reference Shelf

If RefDesk.com wins the blue ribbon for excellence in reference, then the second-place award goes to the "Virtual Reference Shelf" from the Library of Congress. The site may lack the idiosyncratic charm of Dr. Drudge's handiwork, but the elegant and sleek collection of prime reference materials is worth a spot in your growing library of standard sites.

Internet Public Library

The Internet Public Library (ipl2) is a dependable site for reference tools put together by a group of web-savvy librarians. As mentioned in Chapter 4, librarians have long been adept at constructing pathfinders, or brief explanations of how to research specific topics, and ipl2 specializes in them. Pathfinders point the way to resources and search strategies on a variety of topics, and the ones ipl2 provide are superb. If this redoubtable researchers have fashioned a pathfinder for a subject of interest, count yourself lucky. The directory of links to an assortment of reference topics is equally deserving of your attention. As a public service to the researching public, ipl2 is one of the best.

Online Directories

Finally, try the collection of reference sources available from the directory services of Yahoo! and the DMOZ Open Directory Project. Although you may not think of today's Yahoo! as a basic directory of useful web resources, that's where Yahoo! got its start. It still provides a directory, and it's still an excellent place to find helpful reference sites. The Yahoo! directory has plenty of links to standard reference works (dictionaries, encyclopedias, calendars, libraries of quotations, and the like), but it also offers some idiosyncratic links too. Need to check on measurements and units? Statistics? Directories for very specific subjects? Phone numbers and addresses? Yahoo!'s got them.

DMOZ is a crowd-sourced collection of links organized into a logical taxonomy. It may not be as current as Yahoo!, but it still is a viable source for quick reference links.

Finding Additional
Reference Resources

While you zip around the web searching for information, keep track of reference sites of interest. As you no doubt already have realized, reference resources solve one of the basic problems of research, which is knowing where to begin to look. Certainly an almanac isn't the only source you need to master a subject, but it can provide that initial spark of insight. The general-interest reference sources discussed here are good starting places. They save time and money, not to mention frustration. By keeping a sharp eye out for websites that serve as good reference sites, you can become your own reference desk. How do you know what a good reference site is? Remember, a trustworthy site will be current, the publisher or the editor will be authoritative in the subject matter, and the site will be designed for ease of use.

> **Reference resources solve one of the basic problems of research, which is knowing where to begin to look.**

SITES AND SOURCES MENTIONED IN THIS CHAPTER

Bartleby.com
http://bartleby.com

DMOZ
www.dmoz.org

Encyclopaedia Britannica
www.britannica.com

Google Books
http://books.google.com

Google Maps
http://maps.google.com

Infoplease
www.infoplease.com

ipl2
www.ipl.org

Library of Congress's Virtual Reference Shelf
www.loc.gov/rr/askalib/virtualref.html

Math.com
www.math.com

Project Gutenberg
www.gutenberg.org/wiki/Main_Page

The Quotations Page
http://quotationspage.com

RefDesk
www.refdesk.com

ThomasNet
www.thomasnet.com

U.S. Census Bureau's American FactFinder
http://factfinder2.census.gov/faces/nav/jsf/pages/index.xhtml

The World Almanac
www.worldalmanac.com

YourDictionary
www.yourdictionary.com

Associations

We've already seen how Google, when used in conjunction with public databases, can help us find things on our own. But what about those times when we need to have a subject explained to us? Or when we need an expert to show us the way? Or when we need an answer immediately and don't have the time to learn about a subject ourselves? That's where associations come in.

Types of Associations

As a source for information, few things are better than associations because there's an association—or guild or society—for just about everything, no matter how obscure or rarefied. If one single human being embraces a passion or falls in love with some irresistible interest that fires her mind and soul, someone else in this good green world will discover it too. And these two will find each other. It's uncanny how people with similar interests—those proverbial birds of a feather—find one another, and when they do, they form associations. This urge to associate joins death and taxes on the list of life's certainties.

As you will quickly discover, associations exist for activities ranging from the sublime to the unspeakable. Some are formal professional organizations, such as the American Bar Association for lawyers and the American Medical Association for doctors. Others may be industry groups that exist to promote mercantile interests, such as the Corn Refiners Association, the Independent Lubricant Manufacturers Association, and the Association of Apparel and Textile Exporters in Bulgaria. Still others may be activist groups that take a stand on political or social issues, such as MADD (Mothers Against Drunk Driving), the Environmental Defense Fund, and the anti-tax Club for Growth. Many associations are recreational in nature. Consider the Norwegian Canoe Association, USA Badminton Association, and the Brewers Association. Some groups function quite literally as matchmakers: Parents Without Partners introduces the mamas to the papas, and the World Footbag Association dreams of the day in which no one hacky-sacks alone. In short, if you need information on a subject, you can bet that there is an association just itching to lead you down the path to enlightenment.

Not only do associations exist for virtually every imaginable subject but they all share one thing in common: *They know their business*. An association is not merely a bubbly convocation of people who work in the same industry; it is a repository of knowledge for a specific subject and, within the confines of its interest, can be counted on to deliver a credible point of view. Say, for example, that as part of a marketing campaign, you need to know how many women own handguns in the suburban counties of Minnesota. You could try to track down studies yourself, or you could do what experienced researchers do: Pick up the phone, call the National Rifle Association, and ask one of its experts.

> **An association is a repository of knowledge for a specific subject and can be counted on to deliver a credible point of view.**

Associations are A-list go-to sources because they love to answer questions. If you show even the slightest bit of interest in an association's subject matter—on the phone, by email, or even in person—a reputable association will make sure you get to know everything you want. They are nothing if not zealous. Think of associations as the positive, helpful, and interesting flip side to the motormouth at a party who can't stop talking about himself. Associations are great because they'll keep talking if you keep asking.

Consider this tale of an old flag. I came across it while reading the newspaper. The moral of the story will become clear soon enough.

Back in 1992, a Long Island antiques buff named Gary Laube bought an old trunk at an estate sale. He didn't want the trunk; he wanted the antique blanket he saw inside. Yet, when he got the trunk home and started rummaging through it, Laube discovered it held more than a musty old coverlet. Hidden away inside, underneath the blanket, was a tattered old flag. This was no Betsy Ross project, with stars and stripes and patriotic reds, whites, and blues, but a beat-up piece of cloth with a pine tree pictured on it. The flag was American, that much was obvious, but even an experienced antiques hunter like Laube couldn't guess its history. So he set out to find more about his unexpected bonus.

Fast-forward fourteen years, to July 3, 2006, when *Newsday* staff writer Bill Bleyer picked up the story. As Bleyer tells it, what Laube stumbled upon turned out to be an extraordinarily rare, pre–Revolutionary War flag that likely had been flown during the French and Indian War, perhaps in colonial Connecticut. To flesh out his story, Bleyer quoted Whitney Smith, director of the Flag Research Center, who noted, "This is a pre-Revolutionary military color. . . . We don't know of any other pre-Revolutionary pine tree flags," as well as David Martucci, a flag appraiser and former president of the North American Vexillological Association (NAVA), who pegged the value of the flag at $1 million to $2 million.

The discovery of a historic artifact is a fascinating story by itself. But even more interesting, for our purposes, is that peculiar word *vexillological*. Until I read the *Newsday* account of Laube's find, I had no idea the word even existed. And unless you collect yachting pennants for fun, I would guess that it's not part of your everyday vocabulary either. Having never given much thought to flag experts, I figured that Bleyer probably interviewed all two of them for his article. After all, how many flag mavens can this world hold?

As it turns out, loads of them. Using Google to search with the words "vexillology" "association" quickly reveals that there are far more flag fanciers in the world than you'd ever suspect. I discovered a self-contained world of banner buffs hiding in plain sight. In short order, a researcher in need of information about flags—and not just the million-dollar antique variety—will find organizations and individuals for whom flags are not merely something to salute on a flagpole or wave at NASCAR races but the very stuff that makes their hearts flutter. You may not be able to tell a nautical ensign from a regimental banner, but distinguishing them would be a breeze to the members of such groups as the National Flag Foundation and the New

England Vexillological Association, in addition to the aforementioned NAVA. There are even institutions such as the William Crampton Library, named for one of the world's leading vexillologists, and the Flag Institute, a British group of flag wavers who offer collections of reference materials.

This tale of the rare flag and the experts who can testify to its rarity and great worth brings home the point of this chapter: Find the right association, and in one place you'll have experts to quote, guides to additional information, and an attributable source. Good researchers like Bleyer know this reflexively and appreciate just how helpful an association can be when trying to navigate through unfamiliar subjects or highly specialized types of information. This is especially true when your research project involves scientific, academic, or other complex data.

> Find the right association, and in one place you'll have experts to quote, guides to additional information, and an attributable source.

Mining Association Information

What type of information might an association provide? It depends to a great degree on what the aim of the group is—industry representation or political lobbying or informal gathering of fans—and how well funded it is. Associations can provide everything from factual data to opinions. When you need to pick someone else's brain for a change, turn to an association for the information.

111

Advocacy Data

For every political idea, social policy, or disease, an association stands by to explain and defend the cause to the public. Advocacy organizations lobby for changes in the law and send polished spokespeople out to the media to elegantly tell their stories to the public. Take the Campaign for Tobacco-Free Kids as an example. While most believe discouraging children from smoking cigarettes is a laudable goal, the tobacco industry might think otherwise. So with facts, figures, and sound bites as its weapons, the Campaign for Tobacco-Free Kids wages battle against the tobacco industry's $36-million-a-day marketing efforts with some savvy PR of its own, notably at the "Research Center" on the campaign's website. The association serves up "Fact Sheets" packed with information so that reporters, researchers, and advocates for children's health won't have to do the digging themselves.

> **For every political idea, social policy, or disease, an association stands by to explain and defend the cause to the public.**

Need to follow the money in politics? The site's "Tobacco PAC Contributions" reveals into whose pockets all those industry dollars flow. And in the collection of "Special Reports," the campaign offers in-depth analysis of leading issues, such as a report bolstering the idea that higher cigarette prices do in fact reduce consumption. What the Campaign for Tobacco-Free Kids does is no different from what other associations that want to shape public opinion do. They research their special subjects so the public doesn't have to. If they're giving it away, take it.

Energetic advocates like the Campaign for Tobacco-Free Kids stay on top of the news and are excellent sources for timely or even controversial material. In 1998, the attorneys general of several states reached a settlement with tobacco companies over the cost of Medicaid attributed to treating diseases caused by smoking in state hospitals. At the law firm where I then worked, the partner and his team needed me to get a copy of the settlement as soon as it was publicly available. As they reminded me, time was of the essence. The first website to publish the settlement documents didn't belong to one of the parties to the agreement, as you might expect, but to the Campaign for Tobacco-Free Kids, who cared as passionately about the topic as the lawyers did.

Advocacy groups bend over backward to publicize their causes and are delighted to share information with anyone who needs it. They do the no-glamour digging for facts, which they give away in hopes of earning attention for their cause.

Legal advocacy isn't the only type of support associations provide. In their efforts to influence public opinion, associations are inveterate letter writers and paper publishers, issuing white papers that detail their position on social issues. Some groups that speak for a profession, like the National Association of Biology Teachers (NABT), can even define standards for a given discipline. On its website, it's pleased to offer the public access to its position papers. Dear to their professional hearts are topics such as "Equity in Science Education," "Characteristics of Exemplary Life Science Teaching," and "Teaching About Environmental Issues."

Likewise, the Specialty Coffee Association of America shares with the world its "Sustainability Statement": a bullet-pointed aspirational list of what the industry ought to do to encourage environmentally friendly coffee agribusiness. If you need an opinion on public policy, an association can be counted on to provide both the opinion and the facts and figures to back it up.

Facts

For factual information, use your common sense. You don't need me to tell you that the rules of safe boating can be found on the website of the National Safe Boating Council, that the price of gold on February 18, 2010, is available from the London Bullion Market Association, or that the number of registered Republicans in the United States can be verified by the Republican National Committee. Define your problem and think of who would have an interest in providing an answer. A relevant association can usually deliver an authoritative answer very quickly. (In the next section, I'll show you how to locate associations.) When searching an association's website for information, calling its library, or contacting a spokesperson, you'll find associations generally are happy to hand over facts, numbers, and other verifiable details just by asking.

Studies and Reports

Commissioning studies and then writing reports on the results is oxygen to most associations: It's what they do. Any group that can afford a telephone, an office, and a website probably is putting together research for the edification of its members—and the general public. Take a look at the National Association of Counties, which offers county officials guides on social policy. At the moment, it is giving away its surveys on the impact of methamphetamine abuse on local municipalities to help county executives better grapple with drug abuse. Or see what the New Mexico Association of Food Banks says on how to improve the distribution of foodstuffs to needy New Mexicans. What's in it for the association? Publicity, certainly, along with the opportunity to define issues on its own terms and sway public opinion. Plus, in the web era, it doesn't cost anything to put up a link to a document. Information wants to be free, right?

When it comes to white papers, keep in mind the thinking-like-a-detective way of approaching information gathering. The meat and potatoes of the reports is valuable for its own sake, but the good stuff lives in the fine print. Footnotes and bibliographies provide more nuanced explanations and links to additional materials. Track down the quoted experts. Read those studies closely for the additional nuggets of wisdom lurking inside those formal reports. What seems like slogging at first glance is actually sleuthing and frequently pays off handsomely in additional information about your research subject.

Studies may be specially commissioned by an association or written by its staff. Associations are often made up of professionals who produce reports backed by academic credentials and experience in the field. But regardless of the author, associations stand behind their publications, giving you the benefit of an attributable source.

For a textbook example of a helpful white paper, look at "Surgical Management of the Burn Wound and Use of Skin Substitutes." This paper, from the 3,500-member American Burn Association, is interesting in its own right as a description of burns for the benefit of claims administrators at hospitals. In the course of the paper, the authors describe the different types of burn wounds, how they are classified and treated, and what additional treatments may be necessary for the burned patient.

Look closely, though, and the paper also provides the names of experts, specifically the authors; names of institutions specializing in burn treatment; and the contact information for the association spokesman. The names of products used to replace burned skin are mentioned. Surgical techniques unfamiliar to the layperson such as allografting are described. For a researcher looking into any aspect of the treatment of burn victims, this single paper would point to any number of promising additional sources and suggest different avenues for additional search. Mining the incidental data within white papers is the way professional researchers reduce the number of hours of online search and hit-or-miss emails to possible sources.

> **Mining the incidental data within white papers is the way professional researchers reduce the number of hours of online search and hit-or-miss emails to possible sources.**

Statistics

Statistics can paint a vivid picture in numbers. Whether you are a numbers nerd whose heart throbs at talk about means, modes, and medians or a grouch who thinks numbers are as likable as gout, finding statistics is part of every researcher's task. Rather than wading through many pages in search of the percentage that will seal your argument, find statistics galore at an association. In studies, press releases, and daily updates, associations frequently make their case in the language of statistics. Keep an eye out for them.

Quotable Spokespeople

Contact an association to find experts whose opinions hold weight. Even the smallest organizations can provide access to someone with a demonstrable mastery of a subject at best or a passing acquaintance with the topic at least. Larger associations generally have a PR person on staff who can field questions intelligently. The most media savvy will trot out an experienced talking head to dish up a tidy sound bite.

Referrals to Interview Subjects

Not all associations keep their experts locked up in the basement at headquarters. If the person on the receiving end of an email or a phone call can't answer your question himself, pump him for the contact information of someone who can. Well-run organizations usually have boards of directors, which are populated by experts such as academics, business executives, subject matter pooh-bahs, or other brainy worthies who know the subject well and can be counted on to be in a mood to share their expertise with you. *Always* ask an association for contacts or references.

Pointers to Additional Information

So after you've exhausted an association and its staff and harvested every last factoid from the website, what's your next move? Where can you wring even more information out of an association? Keep your eye on the association's website for pages with titles such as "Resources," "Links," and "Library." These gateways are your free ticket to bonus information in addition to what an association itself provides. In New Orleans, they call it *lagniappe*, a little something extra. Don't be shy. Help yourself.

I'll remind you about a handy Google utility that will serve up second helpings of information. Once you locate an association site you like, copy and paste the URL into the search box named for finding pages that link to a page on Google's "Advanced Search" template. If a particular association's webmasters don't deliver the goods, let Google expand your search to similar organizations that might be able to help.

Don't be nervous about asking an association what magazines or books you should be reading to learn about the subject. The larger, better-funded associations may even have an information center or library staffed with a real human being who can help you compile a bibliography. If so, you've hit upon an indispensable resource. Put the librarian's email and phone number in a safe place.

How to Locate Associations

Obviously, before you can begin to mine the rich veins of information an association promises, you have to find the association first. The basic sources and techniques set out in this section will deliver association names and put contact information in your hands with minimal effort. The *Encyclopedia of Associations* is always an excellent starting place, but don't fret if you don't have access to it. Because there are enough other online tools to do the job, access to the encyclopedia is no longer as essential as it once was.

Web Search

Probably the easiest way to locate an association is to run a Google search using the following format:

association "your subject"

This Google search . . .	. . . should produce a link to . . .
association " horseshoes"	National Horseshoe Pitchers Association of America
association "chewing gum"	National Association of Chewing Gum Manufacturers; International Chewing Gum Association
association "tinnitus"	American Tinnitus Association; British Tinnitus Association; Australian Tinnitus Association
association " cosmetics"	Cosmetics, Toiletry and Fragrance Association
association "hiking"	American Hiking Society

If you don't have success locating an association, try other common search synonyms such as "society," "organization," "club," "order," "federation," or "conference." Another good Google technique is to search for your subject and then restrict the search to the .org domain to locate noncommercial sites. You could start with the following search if you were interested in the rules of boating safety:

"boating" site:.org

Web Directories

Feeling lazy and uninspired? It happens to the best of us, and when it does, we deal with it by clicking around search directories. Remember, directories are put together by people, not by computers the way search engines are. If you want to see all the links a topic in one place, without having to do a Google search, the hierarchical directory DMOZ (discussed in the previous chapter) is the answer.

ASAE and the Center for Association Leadership

The principle that people of similar interests will find one another and create an organization also holds true for the people who *themselves* operate and manage associations. The ASAE and the Center for Association Leadership is an umbrella organization made up of the American Society of Association Executives, the ASAE Foundation, the Center for Association Leadership, and the Greater Washington Society of Association Executives. Find the "Gateway to Associations," a database of more than 6,000 member organizations, by searching for "gateway" on ASAE's website.

Joining Associations

As we've seen, associations are extraordinarily generous with their information. Whether you're picking the brain of a spokesperson over the phone or cruising around a website scooping up handfuls of free facts, useful materials are there for the taking. While associations, as a rule, are generous with their information, some do have limits and

> **Associations are extraordinarily generous with their information.**

ENCYCLOPEDIA OF ASSOCIATIONS

For years, librarians have consulted the *Encyclopedia of Associations* to help answer questions when their own workplace collection couldn't. Now in its forty-eighth edition, which attests to its staying power as a standard reference, the venerable encyclopedia continues to provide "detailed information concerning more than 25,000 nonprofit American membership organizations of national scope." Organization profiles feature the mailing address, website, contact person, date of founding, number of members, annual membership dues, and a brief description. If the organization publishes newsletters, books, or reports, the encyclopedia notes that as well. To make searches simple, all associations are grouped according to broad subject areas. For more information, contact the publisher:

Gale
27400 Drake Rd
Farmington Hills, MI 48331-3535

(Yes, you should write them a letter on a piece of paper.) You also should check with your library to see if they have a print copy at the reference desk or a license to the electronic version.

Ten Interesting Associations
As a way to drive home the point that associations exist for even the most eclectic subjects, let's play Association Roulette. The rule (there's only one) is to find arcane associations, by thumbing through the *Encyclopedia of Associations* at random, running random searches through the associations directory from the ASAE and the Center for Association Leadership "Gateway to

Associations," or by Googling any noun that springs to mind in the same search as the word *association*. Humanity is nothing if not diverse in its passions.

American Institute of Organbuilders: For professional builders of pipe organs.

Xerces Society: Its members work for the preservation of invertebrates; named for an extinct species of butterfly.

American Glovebox Society: This group of professionals works with gloveboxes needed in industries in which people work with scary substances such as viruses, radioactive materials, and other stuff that cannot be let loose in the neighborhood.

American Textbook Council: Their chapters take their chapters seriously.

Governors Highway Safety Association: Right turn on a red light? Someone has to decide if it's a good idea.

North American Raspberry and Blackberry Association: Formerly the North American Bramble Growers Research Association. Update your address book.

American School Food Service Association: A group for the lunch ladies, not the ladies who lunch.

Miss Rodeo America Alumni Association: Cowgirls forever.

Long John Silver's Franchisee Association: Servers of fish-and-chips worldwide can dish on the haddock.

International Association for Near-Death Studies: Tracking the experience of anyone who saw the light but said, "Thanks, but no thanks."

> ### TRY THIS AT HOME
>
> To see the power of associations in action, look at how skilled reports weave comments from a variety of associations into their stories. Skim through the top five stories from today's *New York Times* and see how long it takes before you see a quote attributed to a spokesperson for a particular group. Chances are the quote will appear within the first few paragraphs of the story. Reporters understand the importance of backing up stories with attributable quotes, and associations are usually the best place to find qualified spokespeople.

save their most valuable information collections for members. If you really need access to members-only information that the association provides, join it! Members often get access to a list of other members, private blogs, members-only reports, news updates, and subscriptions, and proprietary databases. Of course, not all associations are open to everyone—membership may be restricted to members of a profession, to people working within an industry, or to those who can produce credentials. There are plenty of associations to choose from. Do some diligent digging to find one that will accept you at a price that's right.

SITES AND SOURCES MENTIONED IN THIS CHAPTER

American Glovebox Society
www.gloveboxsociety.org

American Institute of Organbuilders
www.pipeorgan.org

American School Food Service Association
www.asfsa.org

American Textbook Council
www.historytextbooks.org

ASAE and the Center for Association Leadership
www.asaecenter.org

ASAE and the Center for Association Leadership's Gateway to Associations Search
www.asaecenter.org/Directories/AssociationSearch.cfm

Association of Apparel and Textile Exporters in Bulgaria
www.bgtextiles.org/?cid=58

Corn Refiners Association
www.corn.org

Governors Highway Safety Association
www.ghsa.org

Hong Kong Sex Education Association
hksea.3tech.com.hk/chi

Independent Lubricant Manufacturers Association
www.ilma.org

International Association for Near Death Studies
http://iands.org/home.html

Long John Silver's Franchisee Association
www.ljsfab.org

New York Times

www.nytimes.com

North American Raspberry and Blackberry Association

www.raspberryblackberry.com

Xerces Society

www.xerces.org

7

Finding People

Remember rule number one of research: You need to ask a question that can be answered. By Googling a name, you're already following that strategy. When it comes to people searching, an answerable question is a succinct "Who am I looking for?" So whether you realized it or not, by Googling for an ex-flame, you quite naturally started your research by using what you know—the name of the person—to find out what you don't know: his or her current phone number or email or married name or home address or current occupation. You can't find out anything about a person without some rudimentary information to start with. That's almost always a name, preferably one that's accurately spelled. Sure, police track down strangers with little more information than the clues they glean from a crime scene, but we are not the cops. The constabulary has search tools like forensics labs, the National Crime Information Center, and a vast archive of fingerprints with names attached to look through. You and I, however, will need to rely on Google and the contents of this chapter to find the people on our personal most-wanted lists.

When we talk about finding people, we're really talking about finding a person's indicators, the contact information we can use to get in touch with him or, in the case of the deceased, information for a close family member or friend. Factual bits of information like phone numbers, email addresses, and home or business addresses can put us in touch with the object of our investigation, who could be a specific individual or a specific *type* of person. Let's get sleuthing.

When we talk about finding people, we're really talking about finding a person's indicators.

Searching for a Specific Person

It will be tempting to just type a name into Google, but effective people locating is rarely that simple and has its own set of challenges.

Make Sure You Are Looking for the Right Person

The gold standard for personal identification, after a birth certificate, is a driver's license or an equivalent state ID card. However, identifying information contained on a driver's license or in the data concerning a vehicle's registration, discoverable by its license plate, is no longer available to the public. The days are over when anyone could walk off the street into the Department of Motor Vehicles, pay a small fee, provide a license plate number, and then see the name and address of the person who owns that vehicle. The Drivers Privacy Protection Act (DPPA) has been federal law since 1994 and prohibits the release of any personal information contained within driver records to anyone, except for some certain clearly defined uses. Those exceptions are for the use in court proceedings, recall of motor vehicles, and market research. (Private investigators also have an exemption that permits them to get to the IDs.) For a complete explanation of the genesis of the law and the series of rather gruesome stalking cases that led to the enactment of the law, see what the privacy advocates from the Electronic Privacy Information Center have to say about the DPPA.

The best you can hope for, when you have neither a Social Security Number nor a driver's license, is to nail down an address, exact name, a phone number, or other unique identifier.

Unique Names Are Rare

In a nation of 311 million, finding the right edition of the name you're searching for is task number one. Consider how many Jennifers you can name off the top of your head. It's not often that you're going to search for someone with a one-of-kind name, like the former Atlanta Braves baseball player Wonderful Terrific Monds III. Even a name as unusual as Mr. Monds' is now no longer the only one. To get the right person, particularly one with a common name, try to include additional identifying characteristics in your search, such as age, geographic location, or occupation. Even then, take the utmost care to get the correct individual and not someone with the same or very similar name of the person you are looking for. You don't want to be looking for Donald Trump of Greensboro, North Carolina, and instead turn up information about a New York man with implausible hair.

> Take the utmost care to get the correct
> individual and not someone with the same
> or very similar name of the person you are
> looking for.

Spellings Are a Mess

Names are not always spelled the way they sound. Trust me. I once collected junk mail misaddressed to me and counted twenty-seven different misspellings of my last name. As with knowing how to spell a word to look it up in the dictionary, you'll need the correct spelling of a person's name to find her. Even with that, you should understand that many records can be wildly inaccurate themselves. Misentered data, illegible records, and simple misspellings make records containing names unreliable under the best of circumstances. So be warned. There is no simple solution to this problem except to do your best to spell the person's name correctly from the beginning of your research and be ever vigilant for name variations.

Names Change

Maiden names become married names; some birth names are retained professionally after marriage but changed for family and personal uses; some hyphenate the family name; others might change their name from John to Mergatroyd just because they want to. Stay alert to changes in names and be on the lookout for variations on a name.

Someone named Jane Ellen Foster might be known professionally as J. Ellen Foster, but called Ellie by everyone else. Be creative. Not finding John Doe? Try Jon Doe, Johnny Doe, Jack Doe, Jonathan Doe, and any other variation on a person's name you can think of.

Data Are Often Stale

Even the best people-finder services can't keep up with our peripatetic population. You'll routinely find old records, out-of-date addresses, and the names of long-dead individuals popping up in the same results list as vital human beings. Be forewarned that you'll need to be extra-careful with the data you see.

Some People Don't Want to Be Found

For reasons spiritual, marital, or legal, a fair number of people don't want to be found. They choose to live off the grid. If people prefer not to leave the ordinary trails that the rest of us do simply by being a member of society, your hunt may never pan out. And unless you want to become your own private investigator and start working the phones and pressing every contact who ever knew, saw, or spoke to the person, there's not much else to do to gather information on them. One

---

If people prefer not to leave the ordinary trails that the rest of us do simply by being a member of society, your hunt may never pan out.

131

word of advice though. Should you have a last known address for an elusive contrarian, you might be able to skip-trace them. Find the neighbors at the last known address (or job or friend) and contact *them* to see if they might be able clue you in to the person's whereabouts. Don't feel bad if you can't find someone. I don't advocate ever giving up, but sometimes you do hit a dead end simply because the public trail goes cold. If it's important to contact an otherwise unfindable person, turn to professional investigators who have the experience and manpower to look in greater detail.

Research Tools for Finding People

With some caveats established, let's get going by looking at one of the reference tools long used by researchers and now updated for the twenty-first century. May I suggest that you start not with Google but with the phone book.

The Phone Book

The phone book query is the most basic person search of all. Back in the days when landlines were standard and cellphones were giant and found only in Sean Connery–era James Bond movies, phone books were marvelous people finders for one simple reason. In addition to the telephone numbers, phone directories also listed the physical address of where the subscriber was located. It was a snap to find people by phone number alone. So up until the time that cellphones took over the world, reporters, cops, and private eyes routinely started their searches for people in the most obvious place of all: They looked in the phone book. You should too. Names, addresses, and yes, phone numbers come quickly, accurately, and at no cost.

The phone book query is the most basic person search of all.

So before you wrack your brains trying to Google for someone's phone number or address, look him up in one or all of the three major online directories: AnyWho (from AT&T), WhoWhere? (from Lycos), and 411.com (from WhitePages). They load data from phone books across the nation into one giant database; in practice, local city and town phone books are turned into an immense countrywide people finder service. The services are excellent and fast, though some small print exclusions apply. Only individuals who choose to list their phone numbers in the phone book are included, and you will need to know both the correct spelling of the person's name and at least the state (preferably a city) in which the person lives. The listings are for land lines only.

Even with these constraints, there's plenty of research mojo left in looking up people in the phone book. Land lines still count for roughly three quarters of all telephones in the United States; only a quarter of American households are cellphone only. As you might imagine, the split between cellphone only and landline only (or landline primarily) runs along generational lines. The days of landlines and phone books may be numbered, but until that day comes, the old-school phone book search is still a worthwhile gambit.

Cellphones

So what about cellphones? How to do you locate someone's cellphone number? The short answer is that you can't do it reliably. Unlike landlines, cellphones clearly do not need to be assigned to a specific location. Also, privacy laws that never applied to landlines protect cellphone numbers. Still, because the marketplace abhors a vacuum almost as much as it does a dollar fleeing unearned, some companies have stepped into the business of providing cellphone information for a fee. The National Cell Phone Registry is a for-profit service that trolls public records for cellular information and then sells access to its database. Other personal-information data providers, like Intelius, will provide a cellphone number for a fee as well.

We may yet see the day when cellphones will have a repository similar to the phone book database to offer numbers to the public for anyone who chooses to make his cell number available. It will require some regulatory changes and a shift in how our new telecomm networks develop socially, but such a service would certainly be a winner.

Reverse Lookup

Reverse phone lookups correlate a phone with an address. With a phone number in hand, a reverse lookup reports on the name of the number's owner and usually an address as well. If you really want to play detective, you can use these address and phone number searches in conjunction with a map service like Google Maps to search for neighbors of the person in question. In the predigital dark ages, researchers relied on a publication known as the *Coles Directory* for reverse lookups, a process that uses a known phone number to find out who it belongs to. These artifacts of the twentieth century are still useful for historic research, and a handful of libraries may still retain old versions of the directories. This is handy if you have an address for a person who has since moved. Find out who the person's neighbors were and contact them to see if they know where the person you are searching for has gone. This is a technique long favored by skip-tracers and law enforcement to find people who have moved on from their last known addresses.

Reverse cellphone searches are challenging, but the site Lookup a Cell Phone Number will narrow down the geographic region of a given number by reporting on the cell company that provides the service to that number. To get at least a general sense of where the cell number is located, try it. The site won't tell you the name of who owns the number, but it will narrow down the list of potential owners.

Historical Research

Print phone books are on the way out, but if you're conducting research into the recent past, obsolete phone books offer a way to verify addresses of people and businesses from the last century. Bigger libraries will keep a collection of these treasures specifically for the benefit of researchers. Think of how helpful it is to find an address for a person from the 1940s for genealogical research, for instance, or to find the exact name and location of a long-gone business from a really yellowed Yellow Pages directory as a way to verify the history of a particular neighborhood.

People Finder Websites

Let's now move from rotary dial to digital and tune in to a quartet of sites that collect disparate personal data from phone books and public data sources and turn that information into searchable websites. These sites try to overcome the deep web query problems that keep other search engines from dredging up details on individuals.

At the top of the list is Pipl, which pulls together background reports, blog posts, real estate listings, bylines in professional publications, profiles extracted from social media, and a variety of databases that might conceivably contain information about a person. The results are impressive, if a bit of a mess in the hard-to-read display. Spokeo is a deep web service that trains its algorithms at public records sources, which Spokeo describes as "including but not limited to: phone directories, social networks, marketing surveys, mailing lists, government censuses, real estate listings, and business websites." Wink bills itself as the "world's largest people search engine," and as I have no evidence to the contrary, I have no reason to doubt it. Its main draw is its inclusion of non-U.S. citizens, particularly from Canada and the United Kingdom. Zaba Search is a free name-and-number search engine powered by Intelius that in its premium form offers reverse search by phone number, Social Security number search, and background check information for $4.99 for a single phone number.

Last, an interesting piece of programming wizardry is a little add-on for the Firefox browser named Who Is This Person? As the blurb for the download promises, "Highlight any name on a web page and see matching information from Wink, LinkedIn, Wikipedia, Facebook, Google News, Technorati, Yahoo Person Search, Spock, WikiYou, ZoomInfo, IMDB, MySpace and more..." It's a helpful mash-up of personal information from some of the leading producers of factual data.

Google and People Searching

You probably don't need much advice now on the nuts and bolts of how to use Google to locate a person. The best additional advice is to pay close attention to the clues that come up in the results list. While reviewing that list, be aware of hidden references that point to the person you're looking for and that may not be obvious at first glance. An alumni newsletter that mentions the spouse of the person you're

---

GUESS THE EMAIL ADDRESS

Making a good guess at someone's email address can work wonders. Is it jsmith@thejonescompany.com or john.smith@thejonescompany.com or john.d.smith@thejonescompany.com? If you're wrong, the email bounces back. If not, the address is probably a valid one.

---

searching for may be exactly the bit of information that in turn will help you find your quarry. In fact, reading a stray Google document was how I found a long-lost college acquaintance. It had been years since I'd been in touch with "Sarah." I wasn't finding any information in any of the sites we already detailed, and she wasn't even on Facebook or LinkedIn. But then, while sifting through a Google results list, I came across the pdf of a flyer from an elementary school in California. Google doesn't throw documents into its results list just for fun, so that flyer had to have popped up for a reason. Inside the flyer, I saw a passing reference to Sarah. This Sarah had the same name as my friend; she was working as a part-time teacher at the school. That tidbit was exactly the information I needed to take the next steps. With some additional Googling for the elementary school, I found a small bio on the school's website that confirmed this Sarah went to my college and so was likely the one I was looking for. A search through the phone book and a quick spin through Google Maps and I soon had Sarah's home phone number and address. And by looking at the school's website, I could determine the email convention they used so that I could make an educated guess at her email address.

In this instance, an obscure fact snagged from a little publication was all I needed to open the door to what I was looking for. My advice is to read everything.

Google also helps in people searching by turning up references in the press via Google News or biographies of businesspeople in Google Finance. News stories are valuable for helping to pin down a location or an occupation. ("R. A. Ceisler, 55, junior account executive for Worldwide Cheese Distributors in Bellmore, NY, was promoted to senior sales manager.") Such stories can also be valuable for indirect references to the person you want to find. News stories frequently contain references to spouses, relatives, coworkers, or neighbors, which can point you to the right person and offer clues about where to look next.

Social Networks

The explosion of social networking has made it much easier to chip away at those famed six degrees that theoretically separate everyone in the world. The advent of social networking tools has introduced an entirely new way of locating individuals. In a world in which people willingly broadcast their age, gender, marital status, religion, hobby, photos, and formerly intimate personal data, who needs detective skills?

> **The explosion of social networking has made it much easier to chip away at those famed six degrees that theoretically separate everyone in the world.**

Little needs to be said about Facebook. With more than 500 million users worldwide and more being added every day, Facebook is an indispensable tool for finding people. Of even greater interest to a researcher is Linkedin, if only because it is aimed at a professional audience and dispenses with the pictures of backyard barbecues and game updates. By joining Linkedin, you'll be able to search for individuals from many different companies and occupations. And just as Facebook connects friends and families and Linkedin connects colleagues, Classmates is the service to help connect old school chums. This trio of social networking sites covers a broad spectrum of the online population. Use them all when your research requires someone's email address. These services aid in the preliminary part of people searching, which concerns getting the right person. Often you can distinguish Dave Johnson the salesman from Dave Johnson the plumber with a query inside one of these social networking tools. Each is easy enough to use that no additional instruction is required. Join them today if you haven't already.

Vital Records

As a rule, the basic vital records of birth certificate and death certificates are accessible only to the next of kin or others who have a provable legal interest in the documents. These records are maintained by public agencies, but access to them is strictly regulated. Other vital records, which include marriage licenses, divorce decrees, immigration and naturalization papers, and adoption records fall into a gray area. Some states allow access, others don't. To help sort out what you can and cannot obtain, the Centers for Disease Control and Prevention (CDC) publishes *Where to Write for Vital Records*, a guide to each of the state agencies that provide them. It helps you gather the information you need to quickly obtain the records to which you are entitled, by listing the known facts you'll have to provide to get a copy of a marriage license or a death certificate, for example.

Financial Information

For many businesses and certainly for many legal actions, an asset search is an important component of people searching. It is not enough to know where a person lives or what her phone number is. It is frequently important to know what assets an individual controls. Hunting for assets is a hunt for the records that document ownership of certain tangible objects like a house, airplane, car, or boat. We'll talk about public records in Chapter 9, but for the nonce, one of the people-finder search engines will be your best friend for quick access to asset information from public records sources.

> **Hunting for assets is a hunt for the records that document ownership of certain tangible objects.**

Credit reports and bank records are off-limits to the public; only people or businesses with a legally defined purpose can see them. Access may be granted when extending credit, renting an apartment, or screening potential employees. So if you are neither a lender nor a landlord, the best you can do to figure out someone's financial status is make some educated estimates. If you know what a person does for a living, a salary survey from one of the major jobs sites such as Salary.com can reveal a general salary range. (You can ask about three jobs for free before you have to pay for the premium content.) Look into job listing sites like Monster, CareerBuilder.com, and Indeed, which all offer salary estimates for a variety of occupations.

For some broad insight into what particular jobs pay in different parts of the country, query the Bureau of Labor Statistics' "National Wage Data" for more than 800 occupations. Data are displayed by job, region, and state.

The civil service, the military, and other public positions pay according to easily accessible pay grades. Military pay charts from each of the military branches detail pay based on rank and years of service; most federal jobs are compensated according to the Base General Schedule Pay Scale, but more senior or professional positions fall into the Wage Grade or Senior Executive Service scales. A Google search for "civil service salary" and the state or city you're interested in will bring up the compensation for public servants.

Don't overlook industry associations as a source for salary information. Most associations survey their members regularly and compile the data. Some groups will share data with you if you ask.

Investment Filings

The publicly available servers of the Securities and Exchange Commission's EDGAR database can deliver some insight on the wealthy individuals who work for public corporations. Every corporate officer and director must report their transactions in the stock of the company with which they are affiliated. These so-called insider filings are on Forms 3, 4, and 5, and by tracking them you can get an idea of how well the well-heeled are faring. Anyone who is selling 50,000 shares of stock for $85 a share is doing just swell.

It always helps to look into the compensation of a corporation's officers—the salaries and other compensation paid to the five most highly compensated individuals is listed in the 10-K or proxy statement.

Another SEC filing to tip you off to what the moneyed classes are doing is Form 13-D. Any individual or group who owns 5 percent or more of the outstanding stock of a company must tell the SEC, and hence the public, about it by filing a Form 13-D. It's a good way to see how individual investors are loading up on a stock.

Charitable Donations

Organizations that receive charitable donations need to report that source of income on Internal Revenue Service Form 990. Guide-Star has extracted this information from the filings and compiled it on a searchable database. Use its excellent services to see who is giving what to whom. The Foundation Center is another terrific source for the lowdown on philanthropic givers. It provides some minimal contact information for the foundation and general parameters for how much the foundation hands out, but you can safely presume that anyone who donates $500,000 to the Illinois Committee to Save the Ryan Expressway probably isn't hurting for carfare.

Bankruptcies

The word *bankruptcy* comes to us from the Italian for *banca rota*, or "broken bench." The traditional way of removing a tapped-out trader from the marketplace was literally to break the bench from which he conducted business. In the United States, bankruptcy is a more humane, albeit public, process. The documentation of assets and debts are listed in the bankruptcy court filings. To track down bankruptcy filings at these bankruptcy courts, you will need an account with Public Access to Court Electronic Records (PACER). With a PACER account, you will be able to search nationwide for filings by an individual, with significant details about the assets and liabilities involved. Before you start your search, you should know which court to search by determining where the person in question lived at the time of the bankruptcy filing. The filings, especially the exhibits and schedules that accompany the main documents, will contain remarkably detailed financial information.

Searching for Types of People

A people-searching project is not always in pursuit of a single individual. Sometimes you might be looking not for a known person but rather for a *type* of person. Perhaps you need to find a dentist in Cheboygan, Michigan. Or maybe you need to know about licensed airline pilots in Essex County, Massachusetts. Or you're trying to find out how many registered Democrats are in a specific location and need the contact information for each of them. In each instance, you are looking not for a specific person, but for an individual who fits a certain profile: dentist, pilot, Democrat. Thanks to the wonders of publicly accessible databases, searching for types of people—from judges and doctors to criminals and prisoners and everyone in between—has never been easier. The sources and techniques for digging up the dirt on specific individuals overlap with the how-tos for unearthing information about groups. The same tools that help you find members of a group can also provide you with critical clues to people who fit the profile.

> **Thanks to the wonders of publicly accessible databases, searching for types of people— from judges and doctors to criminals and prisoners and everyone in between—has never been easier.**

Licensed Professionals

The easiest people in the world to locate are licensed professionals. Precisely because doctors and lawyers and others in the learned professions need to demonstrate to the wider world their qualifications to practice, licenses are required.

Physicians

Your research into physicians should begin by checking on their licenses to practice. Depending on the state, all doctors must hold a current and valid license to practice; it is the job of the state board of medical examiners to determine if an applicant is qualified to practice as a physician. The license contains the doctor's educational credentials, addresses, hospital privileges, and other pertinent information that a patient would want to know. Associated with the board may be a licensing commission; you can find out through the American Medical Association's links to state medical boards, where you'll also find licensure requirements and statistics.

Now just because a doctor holds a license doesn't mean that he doesn't occasionally mess up. The Drug Enforcement Agency (DEA) publishes "Criminal Cases Against Doctors," which it describes as "a listing of investigations of physician registrants in which the DEA was involved that resulted in the arrest and prosecution of the registrant." It also pursues administrative law cases against doctors that can result in the suspension of their license to prescribe drugs. If you want to make sure that your own doctor hasn't run afoul of the medical board, refer to the medical licensing boards in your state. In New York, for example, the Office of Professional Misconduct and Physician Discipline will display disciplinary information for doctors in the state; California provides the Medical Board of California License Lookup System to help patients check on licenses and public actions taken against a doctor. For links to state medical license lookups, refer to DoctorScorecard.com.

Other Health Professionals

Non-MD medical professionals, such as dentists, chiropractors, osteopaths, and others in the healing professions, are also required to be licensed. Each state has a licensing board for these professions that every practitioner must meet, though the actual requirements vary from state to state. Almost every individual whose occupation pertains to providing a healthcare service—psychoanalysts, social workers, and veterinarians—also must prove his fitness to practice to a licensing office, though some states are less stringent in their licensing than others. A Google search for:

"[profession]" "[state]" "license"

"dentist" "New York" "license" "board" site:.gov

ought to find you a link that will deliver you to the front door of the agency or board that regulates the profession. Enter and conduct your own specific search.

Lawyers and Judges

Throughout the United States, either bar associations, the state courts, or a combination of the two regulate and license lawyers. To locate lawyers with minimal effort, turn to FindLaw's "Find a Lawyer" database, Martindale.com, or simply Google for them. Few JDs shrink from posting information about themselves online, so finding a lawyer is one of the easier research tasks you'll ever encounter. To make sure the lawyer you're looking for is still in good standing, check with the bar association in the state where the lawyer is admitted. If she is not a solo practitioner but is instead associated with a firm, locate the firm and then search the firm's site for biographical information. Unless a lawyer is unusually shy, an extremely rare disease among attorneys, her online biography ought to list the states and courts in which she has been admitted to practice.

> Finding a lawyer is one of the easier research tasks you'll ever encounter.

Certain specialized courts like the august U.S. Supreme Court or those with special subject matter jurisdiction like bankruptcy or tax courts will require a lawyer to be admitted to that court before he is allowed to practice before it. A quick check with the court's clerk will tell you a lawyer's status. To locate the clerks' office, use the federal court directory from the Administrative Office of the U.S. Courts; state courts are linked to the National Center for State Courts.

Judges and Magistrates

It's the rare court that doesn't have a website, and contact information for all the judges and magistrates is a key component of it. If the bio of a judge is missing from the court's site, look up federal judges in the convincingly named *Directory of Federal Judges* (which also contains the venerable *Almanac of the Federal Judiciary*); state judge bios are standard fare in the reference tome *The American Bench*. These books are standard items at any law library. A call to your county law library should get you an answer to your question from the librarian, who will have these books no more than ten steps from the front desk.

Other Occupations

If on a chore-filled Saturday morning, you say hello to the gardener on the way to a massage before you pick up a prescription and get a haircut, you will be dealing with at least four people who, as a condition of their livelihood, obtained a license to practice. In order to practice one of the learned professions, such as medicine or law, a license is obviously required. Society has a significant interest in knowing that a person who holds themselves out as being skilled in the art of removing pituitary tumors or arguing on your behalf in court actually knows what he or she is doing. But the same holds true for other professions, as well. Learning how to cut hair may not require as much post-collegiate study as neurosurgery, but there is a significant public interest in making sure anyone wielding scissors has some degree of skill with them. Because of that, you'll be able to track down the current whereabouts and contact information for many millions of individuals if you know what they do for a living and where they are employed.

State law varies on exactly which jobs require a bureaucratic stamp of approval, but the way to find out is always the same. Spend some time poking around a state's website to find the office of licenses or some similar operation. States also are quirky about which state departments have power over regulating professions, so you will need to do some initial work to find the regulatory agency in charge of licensing professions. For example, check with the state department of education website to verify teacher certifications.

Pilots also require licensure. Information about them, a group the Federal Aviation Administration quaintly calls "airmen," is available from the Airmen Inquiry database. You'll first need to register on the site—it's free—but after that you can quickly pull out records for individuals by searching for a specific name in a particular city or state

Holders of Nonoccupational Licenses and Permits

Licenses are required not only to work in certain occupations but for certain privileges, such as flying a private airplane, owning a horse or a dog, or operating a store that sells alcoholic beverages. Any diligent searcher should go through some of these license databases to obtain addresses and proper names for elusive individuals.

Because we live in a society in which even hanging a neon sign outside your store requires a permit, tracking down information on business owners is a task for which online searching is perfectly suited. The researcher who wants to master the art of knowing who's who in a community will discover that some time spent learning the ins and outs of the state and county boards that oversee buildings, permits, inspections, and the other regulatory needs of a community will pay off quickly. In these public records, you will uncover names, business relationships, and patterns of ownership in a way that no amount of random Googling could possibly provide.

Here's a simple exercise. Be sure to have your camera phone or a notepad with you the next time you visit a grocery store, drugstore, or restaurant. Note the licenses and permits hanging in plain view near the front door. When you get home, locate the website for the agency that issued the permit or license, and I will wager you the site contains searchable data collections for finding other similar documents. These databases of permits and licenses equip the researcher to find out who owns what and, when used in tandem with information gleaned from the company and corporate records that we' talk about in the next chapter, empower citizens to see who's allowed to do what.

Liquor licenses, cabaret licenses, licenses to store chemicals, licenses to own wild animals . . . the list of things that require the payment of a fee and the filling out of a form goes on and on. The benefit to you is that all of these licenses and permits name names. This is very helpful if you happen to be tracking down an old pal who ran off to join the circus to become a lion tamer. (Check with the Animal and Plant Health Inspection Service, a part of the Department of Agriculture, to see if your friend registered with the agency, as all animal exhibitors are required to do.) These are documents and records that can frequently turn up a stray fact like an address or an association with a company or business, which can, in turn, be leveraged into a much more detailed collection of information about the licensee or permit holder. This is the detective part of research we talked about in the first chapter. You're not slogging through some dreary databases. You're sleuthing!

Experts

Part of finding people is finding people with expertise so that they can share with you what they know. When we talk about experts, we're not only talking about Albert Einstein. Experts abound in all fields, and what qualifies a person to be one varies with the discipline. Professor Einstein's work on physics might make him an expert on how much energy is created when matter is transformed, but nowhere in his work will you find a reliable opinion on the best way to make yogurt at home or the value of the Scandinavian defense in chess. Those are not his field. For all Einstein's genius, his opinions hold weight only on very specific subjects.

> Part of finding people is finding people with expertise so that they can share with you what they know.

Experts come in unlikely packages. A teenager who spends eight hours a day with thumbs securely glued to a cellphone may not be able to name the chemical weight of iridium, but you can count on her, in my humble opinion, to be expertly fluent in the telegraphic language of texting. A retired FBI agent may be wise to the ways of the embezzler. And your brother, who spends every waking moment listening to Crosby, Stills, Nash, and Young, may actually have a very good grasp on when they last played the Cow Palace in San Francisco. In short, by broadly defining experts as people with a specialized knowledge in an area, we need not restrict our search for expert opinion to only those who teach at large, expensive universities. The world opens up when we understand how much learning is walking around in people's heads, many of whom don't hold PhDs.

One of the handiest rules of thumb I know for locating experts is to figure out where people whose interests align with what you are looking for hang out online. I put this strategy to good use once when I was struggling to solve a tough question posed to me by a lawyer. He said there was a word that meant to "go back and forth like oxen plowing a field." He was drafting a document and wanted to use the word to describe the action of a printer head as it moved back and forth across the page, printing one line of text when it zipped from left to right, then printing the next line when it made its return trip from right to left. He was sure such a word existed; the problem was, he couldn't remember what it was. Could I find it for him?

Umm, sure. I diligently checked dictionaries and powered up the search engines, I asked my colleagues and called the New York Public Library, but it was all for naught. Just as I was running out of ideas for places to look, it occurred to me that there had to be a group of people who liked unusual words somewhere online, which is to say, a group of experts. So I logged on to Google Groups, an email-delivered bulletin board service that lets people with similar interests communicate with one another. I turned up a group known as "alt.English .usage" where people who enjoy curious English words can share their love of the mother tongue. So I posted the oxen-plowing-a-field question to the group as a last-ditch effort and left for lunch. To my delight, when I came back an hour later, I discovered twelve responses to my question. "It's boustrophedonic!" they all said. Oh, really? I wasn't going to take the word—literally—of some nameless nerds on the Internet. But when I opened the *Oxford English Dictionary* and looked through the magnifying glass at the 4-point type under "boustrophe-don," what do you know? ". . . alternately from right to left and from left to right, like the course of the plough in successive furrows." Eureka! I reported back to the lawyer. To him, I looked like a brilliant researcher who magically plucked an answer from thin air. The truth of it, of course, is much less exalted. I just knew where to find the right people to ask. The ability to tap into the expertise of other people is a very powerful tool. Find the expert, find the answer.

Find the expert, find the answer.

Asking groups of strangers to help solve your thorny research problems is not some fly-by-night technique used only by desperate librarians. No less an authority than the *New York Times* does the same thing. It recently cast its bread upon the cyberwaters by asking for help identifying the unknown photographer who created a portfolio of World War II photos, including close-up pictures of Adolf Hitler in Hungary. The *Times* posted the photographs on its *Lens* blog (and on a blog hosted by the German magazine *Der Spiegel*) and asked readers to send in their thoughts about who might have taken them. As the *Times* itself reported, "World War II Mystery Solved in a Few Hours." The photographer, identified by a German PhD student named Harriet Scharnberg, was photojournalist Franz Krieger from Salzburg, Austria. Again, eureka. The idea of crowdsourcing information is an interesting one. It's not 100 percent reliable, but when it works, it can pay handsome dividends.

There are other places where you can find experts, and several are mentioned and highlighted throughout this book. Other chapters provide more details on how to extract useful information about people from specific sources. There are smart people all over who will be happy to tell you what they know, and those sources can help you find them.

Criminals

One positive thing to say about criminals—once they've been sentenced to prison, they're easy to find. State jailers and the Federal Bureau of Prisons now offer searchable inmate locators. These databases will help you find the facility in which a prisoner is housed and usually some additional information such as the nature of the crime for which the individual has been jailed as well as the tentative date of his release or parole hearing. The California Department of Corrections, for example, will inform you that inmate #B33920, one Mr. Charles Manson, is currently a resident at the California State Prison at Corcoran and shall be for the foreseeable future. After prisoners are released from custody, many states report on where they have been paroled to, as a service to the broader community.

Similarly, the National Sex Offender Registry coordinates with the databases operated by each state to obtain information on individuals who have been convicted of sex-related crimes and released back into society. It includes names, aliases, and current post-incarceration addresses. For example, Florida operates the Florida Offender Alert System, which allows subscribers to sign up for email notification if an offender or predator moves close to a designated Florida address, such as a residence, office, or school.

Famous People

The problem with tracking down celebrities, like movie stars, rock stars, athletes, and others whose names and faces are known to the world, is that they're besieged by fans. And unlike most of us ordinary mortals, the famous take pains to protect their privacy. In certain cases, they keep their personal lives out of the public eye owing to a sensible concern for the safety of themselves and their families. But it's not impossible to track down the famous; you'll need to work

---

It's not impossible to track down the famous; you'll need to work through intermediaries— namely, their agents or publicity people.

---

through intermediaries—namely, their agents or publicity people. And you should have a good reason to want to talk to a celebrity other than to have a friendly chat or say how much you loved his last movie. From afar, celebrities live magical lives of glamour and leisure; the truth close up is that most brand-name celebrities work extraordinarily hard, and their time is very limited. I learned this during my brief post-collegiate stint as a publicist, when I got to see Hollywood on a workday. The daily grind of making a movie is about as glamorous as steam cleaning the subway.

So to find out who a celebrity's "people" are, check the agent websites. WhoRepresents? and its sister sites, WhoRepsMusic? and WhoRepsSports?, are paid services whose subscribers can search the extensive database of representatives, agents, and PR professionals, many of whose clients are household names. You may never get Lady Gaga herself on the phone, but you could probably talk to someone in her entourage.

The Dead

The departed are still with us. This is neither metaphysics nor encouragement to believe in spooks but an acknowledgment that archives and records survive the departed. Those who now sing in the celestial choir left behind a record of their passage through this wicked world. To a great extent, the field of tracking down the details of peoples past is dominated by genealogists, amateur and professional. To serve these audiences, services have arisen that are essentially interesting compilations of public records and historic account. Among them are some familiar reference titles, some fairly new databases, and, for anyone with a research budget, commercial services that put together all known public records and make them accessible for a fee.

Obituaries

Thanks to its ability to search the text of newspapers, Google does a fair job of fetching obituaries. Search for the name of the departed and the word "obituary" or "obit" or the phrase "survived by," and you can generally find a person's final news report.

Obit Central is an inexpensive service that culls information from cemetery records, obituaries, death notices, and census and immigration records dating to the 1700s; it offers more than a billion data items for you to search. The Obit Central home page provides a search screen, a subscription form, and, more interesting, a collection of links to other subscription research services into the dead, such as Find-a-Grave. Given the amount of time and legwork these sites can save, the minimal annual subscription is a bargain. But if you prefer not to subscribe, try searching the Newspaper Archive for obituaries.

One curious website that is surprisingly not morbid, given its slant and subject matter, is *Obit* magazine, a site that is dedicated to the discussion of death. In addition to its excellent editorial coverage of issues related to the final voyage, it's a good place to find obituaries on the celebrated.

Social Security Death Index

The Social Security Death Index is the final resting place for 87 million-plus former Social Security number holders. RootsWeb, a service of the for-profit Ancestry.com, provides more than 90 million records of deceased Social Security cardholders. The database is intuitive to use, but consult the guide "Tracing Family Trees" for limitations on the records contained in the service, especially missing records.

Who Was Who

The familiar set of biographies known as *Who's Who*, from Marquis, also includes a compendium of past notables in volumes titled *Who Was Who*. The capsule biographies are useful guides to basic facts about the dead.

Genealogy Resources

Genealogists have turned the search into family heritage into an engaging hobby for people curious about their antecedents. A number of genealogy sites will provide instant access to an immense range of data that would take hours of research to put together yourself from the available records. The list of resources from ProGenealogists is probably the best of the bunch, but Ancestry.com and MyHeritage .com are go-to sources for auld folks too. They all charge fees for access.

Veterans

You'll have to get up pretty early in the morning if you want to outdo the U.S. Department of Defense (DoD) in the race to build a vast bureaucracy. The DoD maintains extensive records on all military personnel. To obtain military records, try the automated system from the National Archives and Records Adminstration known as eVet-Recs. You can request records if you are a veteran yourself or if you're next of kin to a deceased service member. However, limited amounts of information can be released to the general public under the Freedom of Information Act by following a process described in detail by the National Archives. One note of caution: A fire in 1973 at the National Personnel Records Center in St. Louis destroyed more than 16 million official records, which had been neither microfilmed nor copied. Many of the records lost to the fire were for army personnel who had been discharged between 1912 and 1960 and air force personnel from 1947 to 1964, meaning many World War I, World War II, and Korean War army records have to be reconstructed from other sources. Handily, the National Archives recommends some alternate sources to help re-create records in response to requests.

Library Resources

The library is still a viable option for people searching. You'll find the average reference collection abounds with books dedicated to looking up information on people.

> **The library is still a viable option for people searching.**

Marquis' *Who's Who*

Perhaps the best-known set of capsule biographies is the *Who's Who* volumes from Marquis. With a collection that it estimates lists more than 1.4 million names, Marquis equips libraries with a searchable database for use by their patrons. The bio entries feature birth date, education, professional career highlights, awards, memberships, contact information, and personal details such as religion and family. The print collections include titles for specific disciplines: *Who's Who in America, Who's Who in American Art, Who's Who in American Law, Who's Who in Corporate America,* and others.

The Social Register

Only people rich enough to use the word *summer* as a verb and droll enough to list the name of their yacht next to the names of their children make their way into the *Social Register*. Well, even a cat can look at a queen. Any researcher curious about where J. P. Stinkingrich and the Mrs. maintain the "dilatory domicile," as a summer estate is known, can waltz through the cotillion of data compiled in this entertainingly pretentious phone directory. It's a standard title at most libraries.

Commercial Services

Businesses and institutions with budget money for public records research can simply buy data from companies that have already done the tedious legwork of contacting county, state, and federal clerk offices and compiled public record profiles of individuals. For those who can afford the search, a number of companies deliver data in a fraction of the time it would take you to undertake the schlep, electronic or otherwise, that is normally required to adequately exhaust the public information compilations. Professional researchers and librarians have long relied on Accurint and KnowX (both are now part of Lexis), and AutoTrackXP (part of Thomson Reuters CLEAR platform for investigations) to divine what is known about an individual.

MY FLORIDA LICENSE

Florida has one of the nation's easiest to use databases for checking on licenses issued within the state. The Department of Business and Professional Regulation offers one-stop shopping for inspection of licenses, something the department calls "Instant Public Records." In a single click, any citizen can see records on everything from elevator permits to the licenses granted to athlete agents. It is a model of public access that other states would be wise to emulate. See the entire inventory on its website, and then check your own state to see if it offers anything remotely as convenient.

Company and Business Research

Factual data about companies, and the industries in which they operate, has never been easier to come by, thanks to the generosity of government agencies, commercial publishers, and the companies themselves. It is a golden age for anyone who needs to track down data on companies.

When we talk about company research, we're talking about a wide variety of disparate information. *Company research* is a generic phrase that encompasses locating financial information about a business, finding biographical information on the honchos who either run or are advisers to the operation, digging up stock market information, compiling news, and gathering together all the other discrete pieces of information that provide a vivid picture of how a company operates.

Entire books could be written on corporate research, so in the interest of brevity, we will cut a few corners here. But even if we won't cover the entire waterfront, by bookmarking a handful of sites and mastering a few corporate research techniques, you'll be ready to scale the corporate ladder of information with something more reliable than just a smile and a shoeshine.

Even if you're not a reporter for the *Wall Street Journal*, knowing how to dig up company information is often valuable for nonbusiness research projects. You may harbor no particular interest in the details of the software business, but knowing the salaries of the executives of the major companies is exceedingly useful if you are a real estate agent with a house to sell in Silicon Valley. If you want to convince a large oil company to stop drilling in the middle of dolphin breeding grounds, it would be helpful to have a source for the company's legal name, state of incorporation, mailing address, and the correct spelling of the CEO's name. And what if you were writing your long dreamed-of book about classic kids toys? Wouldn't it be a big help to be able to locate the spokespeople from Poof-Slinky Inc. (makers of the Slinky) or Wham-O (the Frisbee) or Atari Incorporated (Pong)? Answers to many nonbusiness questions can be found in the documents, reports, and legal filings that businesses of all sizes must produce.

**The first step in all company research
is to determine the type of company
you are looking at.**

The first step in all company research is to determine the type of company you are looking at. Companies fall into four broad categories: publicly held (Microsoft Corporation, Walmart), privately held (Vinny's Pizza, Cargill), nonprofit (American Cancer Society, United Way), and non-U.S. companies (Nokia, Toyota Motors, China Mobile).

Each category offers its own resources and limitations, and the quantity and quality of information available for each one ranges from overwhelming to paltry. On the generous side of the spectrum is information about publicly held U.S. companies. It's easy to obtain and so plentiful that the hard part is making sense of it all (but we shall). On the other end of the research continuum, where the information resources turn rarefied, pinning down even the merest shreds of data about certain privately held foreign companies is close to impossible. Because the sources and techniques of corporate research depend very much on which type of company you're researching, be clear about what you need to find out from the beginning. Remember, the first rule of research is to know what it is you're looking for.

Public Companies

Congress reacted to the stock market crash of 1929 by passing the Securities Act of 1933 to regulate the issuance and sale of securities. Then a year later, Congress created the Securities and Exchange Commission (SEC) with the passage of the Securities Exchange Act of 1934, giving it the enforcement muscle to regulate the market in securities and power to enforce the Securities Act. Ever since the 1930s, the SEC has been the overseer of Wall Street, charged with keeping the stocks-and-bonds racket on the level.

Just how does the SEC keep the moneyed mobs in line? The main way it enforces fairness in the marketplace is by guaranteeing equal access to information, through a very elaborate *disclosure* system. This system requires companies that sell stocks or bonds to the public to file intricately detailed information about themselves and the securities they peddle to investors. The theory makes sense: By making information about a company, good or bad, as accessible to Mary Main Street as to the sharks of Wall Street, the SEC keeps U.S. markets transparent.

This policy of disclosure is as simple as it sounds. Companies that raise money by selling stocks or bonds to the public need to follow the SEC rules and regulations dictating what companies must tell the world about themselves. In practice, as you might imagine, the process is not so simple. The rules and regulations governing the disclosure system that the SEC promulgates are extremely complex. Many a Harvard Law School graduate has paid off his house in the Hamptons by advising corporations on the intricacies of the disclosure rules and then drafting the documents that are ultimately made available to the public to satisfy the disclosure requirements.

Three hard copies of these filings were once sent to the SEC's headquarters in Washington, DC, where the public could look at them in the Public Reference Room. This disclosure system has since evolved into EDGAR (Electronic Data Gathering and Retrieval), which went online in 1995, to both collect filings from companies and to then make those documents available to the public. And here is where the bounty of free information can be harvested: With only a few exceptions, all the information that companies must provide to the SEC is available now, for free, directly from the SEC. Once you open the EDGAR database, you'll have at your disposal a collection of tens of millions of documents filed by the approximately 20,000 publicly held companies, American and foreign, that are subject to the disclosure laws.

And just what will you find in these documents? *Loads.* The alert researcher can unearth an immense array of interesting data about a company from these filings, including:

- The names and salaries of the five highest-paid executives

- How much the company pays (or doesn't pay) in income taxes

- Where the company has factories or offices

- Subsidiaries and percentage of ownership of those subsidiaries

- Financial data—revenues, liabilities, earnings currently and in the past

- Legal documents—the company's articles of incorporation, by-laws, indentures, and employment contracts with key executives

- Industry risks

- Basic directory-style information—names, addresses, and phone numbers of the senior management

- Pending or current lawsuits

Even if your research doesn't require looking at business information per se, familiarizing yourself with EDGAR and learning how to comb through its documents are critically important. A fortune of factual information about companies and the people who run them lies within this stodgy website of seemingly arcane and dry-as-dust documents. Let's lay some groundwork and then take a tour of documents that can yield a stunning amount of information to anyone willing to brave the legalese to help themselves to the facts that the SEC is just giving away.

> **Familiarizing yourself with EDGAR and learning how to comb through its documents are critically important.**

About EDGAR

For all of EDGAR's complexity and the sheer size of the database, searching it is actually straightforward. With a little practice you'll be filling up your hard drive with all the annual reports and proxy statements it can hold.

Access EDGAR from the home page of the SEC by clicking on "Search for Company Filings." Select "Company or fund name, ticker symbol, CIK (Central Index Key), file number, state, country, or SIC (Standard Industrial Classification)." From there, the searching is fairly intuitive.

What intimidates newcomers is the breathtaking volume of form types, most of which make zero intuitive sense whatsoever. But don't fret. To keep things simple, we'll ignore the really specialized filings and focus on the most helpful (10-K, 10-Q, 8-K, and proxy) as well as filings for stock and bond issuances. The first thing to understand is that the filings are organized by company name; the SEC calls companies "issuers" because they issue securities.

COMMERCIAL EDGAR SERVICES

If you, or the company you work for, need to look at EDGAR documents regularly, I recommend getting a subscription to a commercial EDGAR service. These services do a better job of delivering the goods than the SEC does. The companies that repackage EDGAR filings for easier search and retrieval are KnowledgeMosaic, Intelligize, and Accelus (formerly Westlaw Business). Contact them for pricing and details about their services.

Search by company name or ticker symbol, and be sure to *exclude* Ownership Forms 3, 4, and 5. These are forms that the company's officers, directors, and other affiliated parties must file with the SEC every time they buy or sell shares of the company stock. When Bill Gates sells 1,000 shares of Microsoft, for example, he has to tell the SEC about it. The numbers of these forms are legion and are of interest mostly to serious investors who want to be the first to know what the inside money is doing and then divine their intention by reading the tea leaves of insider filings. With these pesky filings eliminated from your search, the results will be a nifty table, sorted in reverse chronological order with the most recent filing on top.

Before we look at specific types of documents, it's helpful to understand a few things about the filings themselves. Most filings are divided into two parts, *base* documents and *exhibits*. Base documents contain whatever information the law requires. In most instances, when a company is required to make certain types of documents— such as contracts, press releases, and transcripts of analyst calls— available, this additional material is appended as an exhibit. To make for easy reference, each base document contains an *exhibit index* to indicate what precisely is being filed as an attachment. Companies that have been around for a while, dutifully filing their documents, can *incorporate by reference,* meaning that rather than provide a required exhibit, they can instead merely refer to a previously filed document so they don't have to file the same items more than once. Typically, an older established company like General Electric doesn't have to file its by-laws every time it delivers its annual report on Form 10-K. It can, instead, simply say, "3(ii) The By-Laws, as amended, of General Electric Company (Incorporated by reference to Exhibit 3(ii) of General Electric's Current Report on Form 8-K dated February 14, 2011 (Commission file number 001-00035))." The prose is not in contention for a Pulitzer Prize, but it gets the job done.

EDGAR filings are broadly grouped into two distinct categories: documents that must be filed according to a set schedule and those that need to be filed when something out of the ordinary happens, such as when a company issues stock or is the subject of a takeover attempt. Generally speaking, the regularly scheduled periodic reports are called '34 Act filings, after the Securities Exchange Act of 1934, which mandates them. When a company chooses to sell a security such as a stock or bond to the public, the requisite filings are known as '33 Act filings, after the Securities Act of 1933, which prescribes those. Think of the '34 Act filings as the routine, dependable annual and quarterly reports and the '33 Act filings as the documents filed when the company does something interesting.

Another category of documents, known as Williams Act filings, are chiefly of interest to investors and are concerned with mergers, going private transactions, takeover attempts, and proxy fights for control of a company. For the general researcher, the greatest value is found in the fact-packed '34 Act filings. The diligent business researcher who needs to dive deeply into the financial arcana of public companies shouldn't just stop with the major filings discussed here but should become acquainted with the entire bestiary of SEC forms. That's a monumental task given the vast array of forms that public companies large and small must file. Refer to the SEC's site for details on the more exotic filings.

> **Think of the '34 Act filings as the routine, dependable annual and quarterly reports and the '33 Act filings as the documents filed when the company does something interesting.**

SEARCHING EDGAR

To open the door to the millions of documents filed on the SEC's EDGAR server, select "Search for Company Filings" from the home page. Once the page opens, click on "Company or fund name, ticker symbol CIK (Central Index Key), file number, state, country or SIC (Standard Industrial Classification)."

Normally, you'll get accurate results by searching for company name. For a more precise search, use the company's ticker symbol. (A link is provided on the site to look up symbols.)

More advanced researchers use the CIK, which is helpful when an issuer has many filings made by subsidiaries with similar names. The CIK is a unique identifier.

Use the SIC search to generate a list of companies that operate in a specific industry.

Important Company Filings

For the disclosure system to work effectively, the SEC needs to think up lots of different forms for lots of different reporting requirements. At first glance, the list of forms looks overwhelming. (At second glance, it looks just as overwhelming.) Nevertheless, the vast majority of filings hold zero interest to anyone except the company, its lawyers, and some investment analysts on Wall Street. You should do just fine by searching for the important filings discussed in this section. For an overview of what the different EDGAR forms do, see "Descriptions of SEC Forms" on the SEC website.

Form 10-K

What is it? The annual report, pursuant to Section 13 and 15(d) of the Securities Exchange Act of 1934.

When is it filed? The 10-K is due ninety days after the end of the company's fiscal year.

What can you find in it? If you had to pick one single EDGAR document to provide the best portrait of a company, you'd choose Form 10-K. This is the annual report—a decidedly nonglossy look at what the company is and does.

If you had to pick one single EDGAR document to provide the best portrait of a company, you'd choose Form 10-K.

The form itself is broken down into four parts, which, in turn, offer information in a standardized format, item by item. For any researcher who needs to check up on a company, learning what's in the 10-K is a key skill. Reading through the contents of a 10-K, and most EDGAR documents, is a way to gather useful facts about a company.

THE COVER

The cover page of the 10-K provides a wealth of information. At the top are the company's formal legal name, its primary business address and phone number, and the jurisdiction in which it is incorporated. Read more closely, and you'll find its number of outstanding shares of common stock. Multiply that number by the price of the stock at today's close, and—voilà!—you've got the company's all-important market cap(italization). There is also some legal mumbo jumbo with checkboxes that everyone but the company's lawyers can ignore without prejudice.

PART I: BUSINESS INFORMATION

In Part I, Form 10-K requires a company to tell the world what it does for a living and disclose the major risks to its business. Properties the company owns are detailed, as are pending lawsuits and any little quibbles that the company might have with the SEC over its EDGAR documents. "Item 1. Business" is the elevator pitch that summarizes the company's entire reason for existing and describes what it produces in its attempt to chase a profit.

Whatever might prevent a company from making a profit or even staying in business or, as the lawyers say, might cause "actual results to differ materially" from the expected ones are set out in "Item 1A. Risk Factors." Companies must identify hurdles, such as change in demand, dependence on a single customer, and difficulties obtaining raw materials. These risks will vary from one industry to another, but the risk-factor text does offer a bracingly honest assessment of the troubles every company needs to overcome.

When companies dispatch their EDGAR filings to the commission, the SEC staff reviews them to make sure that the disclosure documents have complied with the extremely complex disclosure laws. Should the SEC, in its capacity as advocate for the securities owner, not appreciate the way a company has disclosed certain information, it can send a document back with a request for clarification. If the company and the SEC can't hash out the differences, the company needs to let the public know about it in "Item 1B. Unresolved Staff Comments."

Got land? Got a factory? Got lots of leases? "Item 2. Properties" parcels out the real estate.

In "Item 3. Legal Proceedings," companies need to disclose any big-time lawsuits in which they are involved (but not the ordinary run-of-the-mill disputes that every company faces). This is where the company needs to let the world know if the shareholders are suing or if there is some other legal action that may create a substantial liability for the company, which could mean a costly payout or settlement. Think asbestos, oil spills, class action lawsuits, and the like.

Stockholders get their due in "Item 4. Submission of Matters to a Vote of Security Holders." Stockholders, remember, are the owners of a company. As owners, they have a right to vote on certain matters that affect the corporation. If the corporation faces an issue that requires the vote of a shareholder—approval of a merger, say—this is where such information needs to be reported to the public.

PART II: FINANCIAL INFORMATION

For anyone interested in assessing a company's fiscal health, Part II is the place to hear the news from Mahogany Row. As you might be able to discern from the items contained within this part of Form 10-K—"Selected Financial Data," "Quantitative and Qualitative Disclosure About Market Risk"—this is where the corporation accounts for its previous fiscal year in the language of business: syncopated balance sheets and iambic accounting, all of the financial reporting lyrically telling its shareholders just how well the company did (in good years) or explaining why the A for effort balances out the F for results during the lean ones. Because I'm not an accountant, I will not proffer any more advice other than to recommend reading through the various items reported in Part II to get a complete picture of the company's financial status. Remember Enron? Remember WorldCom? Closer reading of Part II might have held clues about the big busts.

If you're not a certified public accountant, your eyes may droop when the dinner table talk turns to FASB statements and the latest news about generally accepted accounting procedures, but the alert researcher who knows the basics of business accounting can find some insight on the interesting ways that companies can tell the world about their incomes, outflows, and prospects for the future. Items 5 to 9B are where the company bean counters have their chance to shine.

PART III: CORPORATE GOVERNANCE

After the money part comes the people part. Part III is like the program at a baseball game: It tells you who the players are, in this case the officers, the senior executives running the operation, and the directors, the outsiders who oversee the company's operation and provide big-picture advice to the officers. In this section you'll be able to locate the names of the insiders, a little professional biography of each one, and, in the case of the five most highly compensated individuals, how much salary, stock, and other compensation they were paid. Directors are also compensated for their services, labor that consists of attending a few meetings per year and delivering advice. Although this compensation must be disclosed in Form 10-K, in practice most companies will incorporate this by reference to their current proxy statement.

Go to town on Part III if you want the juiciest gossip. Sort out the interlocking directorates to see who is supposed to be fully independent but who is actually related to whom, corporately speaking. Find out who in the company is getting big stock options and how big they can cash in if the stock price goes up. Certain salaries are set out here, and you can see what fees the company paid to its accountants. You may have to dig through some previously filed documents to get all the information you want on company insiders, but the scavenger hunt can pay off in learning about how the company is actually run.

PART IV: EXHIBITS AND FINANCIAL STATEMENT SCHEDULES

For the business researcher, the plum information lives in the documents appended as exhibits to the main documents of Form 10-K. These exhibits are like a corporation's legal filing cabinet of important documents; it's where you can locate the fundamental papers of corporate existence, such as the articles of incorporation and the by-laws. You can also indulge in some interesting reading by browsing the employment contracts between the senior executives and the company to see what kind of deal the two parties have made. In the exhibits, you'll also find financial agreements, such as indentures, merger agreements, and amendments to existing agreements. Business researchers, financial pros, and investors are the main audience for these items; for complete scrutiny of a company's operation, diligent researchers know to look through the documents included as exhibits because so much detail is provided in them that doesn't fit neatly in the base Form 10-K.

> **Exhibits are like a corporation's legal filing cabinet of important documents.**

Form 10-Q

What is it? A quarterly report, pursuant to Sections 13 or 15(d).

When is it filed? Forty-five days after the end of the company's fiscal quarter. Fourth quarter results are filed on Form 10-K with the annual wrap-up so only three quarterly reports come out each year.

What is it? The quarterly report tots up the results from the prior thirteen weeks of work. Should something interesting happen that requires additional notice but doesn't warrant inclusion on a Form 8-K, the filing can be appended on Form 10-Q.

Public corporations take their pulses every thirteen weeks to monitor how the business is doing and share that information with the wider world. Every quarter, companies publish the profits and losses for the preceding season, as well as any important documents and agreements the company might have signed during that time. Turn to the 10-Q for the freshest report on a company's financial status.

Form 8-K

What is it? The current report form that's filed whenever anything out of the ordinary happens that the public needs to know about and that can't wait until the next scheduled filing.

When does it come out? Within four business days after a specific event occurs.

What can you find in it? The information on Form 8-K is a hodgepodge of reportable events, so you'll never know exactly what you'll be getting until you look.

The SEC has identified dozens of events that trigger the obligation to file the form. By filing a Form 8-K, a company formally notifies the world that the company filed for bankruptcy or changed the way it accounts for its business or—under the catch-all Item 8.01—reports on any odd occurrence that might affect the company, its share price, or its competitive position. Look to the 8-K for press releases on urgent subjects, announcements of takeover attempts, or public acknowledgment that the SEC is investigating the company. Some of the items requiring disclosure on 8-K are very technical, but these disclosures shed light on the way a company operates and will inform you of interesting and perhaps unexpected events as they occur.

> Look to the 8-K for press releases on urgent
> subjects, announcements of takeover
> attempts, or public acknowledgment that the
> SEC is investigating the company.

DEF 14A

What is it? Definitive proxy statements are documents sent to shareholders to solicit votes for any corporate action requiring shareholder approval.

When does it come out? The routine proxy invitation to the annual meeting comes out, not surprisingly, once a year.

What can you find in it? In addition to routine voting matters, such as for or against a slate of directors, proxy statements are useful for finding executive compensation and information about business relationships.

The proxy statement is routinely sent once a year to all shareholders to invite them to the annual meeting, a standard procedure for corporations throughout the nation. Proxies also are sent during a battle for control of a company, known as a *proxy fight*. In EDGAR, proxy statements are referred to as DEF 14A or DEFA 14A (for definitive proxies) or PRE 14A (for preliminary proxies). The numbers refer to the sections of the Securities Exchange Act that mandated their use.

During a proxy fight, proxy statements are regularly filed with the SEC and sent to shareholders over the course of the contest. Anytime something comes up that requires shareholder action, a proxy statement is sent to the holders. Proxy statements tend to be written in fairly plain English, unlike the other filed forms, which trend toward legalese, and so offer a clearer picture of a company's financial status that's easier to understand than the financial reports in Form 10-K.

Securities Filings

When you or I need money, we might call on friends, relatives, or the nearest friendly bank. When a large corporation needs money, it either sells its shares on the stock market or tries to borrow interesting sums from the capital markets in the form of bonds or debentures or notes, which are all fundamental evidence that someone has lent the corporation money at a certain interest rate for a certain amount of time.

So you know exactly what it is that you are getting when you buy an equity security (a share of common stock, a preferred share, or some hybrid, like an interest certificate) or a debt security (bond, note, debenture, or some other interest-bearing security), the issuing company must provide anyone who asks with a prospectus. This is the legal document that describes the rights of the purchaser and the obligations of the issuer. When you buy a share of Microsoft, you obviously don't actually put a piece of the company in your pocket. Instead you get documented evidence of your purchase.

Before a company can start selling stocks or bonds, it first has to register with the SEC. The registration statement is an exhaustive collection of information, with an emphasis on the company's history.

Registration Statements

A company that is selling securities to the public for the first time, known as the *initial public offering* (IPO), must complete a lengthy form (Form S-1 for a U.S. company, Form F-1 for a company domiciled outside the United States) containing the company's legal documents and years of financial data. Legal documents include the articles of incorporation, bylaws, and any material contracts that could affect the company by requiring it to do certain things (like pay the CEO remarkable amounts of money). The statement itself is a thorough review of the company, its management, and the industry in which the company operates, presented in exquisite detail. The text is dense legalese, but plow through, and you'll be treated to a complete and fact-filled tour through the inner workings of the soon-to-be public company.

The registration statement is first reviewed by examiners from the SEC to make sure that it is accurate and complies with all the required disclosure laws. Once the SEC has pronounced the registration to be in compliance with its regulations, the agency gives the company the thumbs up to sell its stock or bonds by issuing an effectiveness order. The effectiveness order tells the world that the registration has passed legal muster and that the company can legally sell the security to whoever wants to pay for it (with certain rare exceptions).

Once the company has its initial offering under its belt and has satisfactorily complied with all of the SEC's requirements, filings for subsequent issuances of stocks or bonds can be made on considerably shorter forms. Issuers of long standing who are responsible corporate citizens (from the SEC's point of view) are permitted to use Form S-2 or F-2 (which allows for some incorporation by reference) or Form S-3 or F-3 (which allows for maximum incorporation by reference).

Once the registration statement has been finalized, the issuer can begin to sell the securities on the open markets. The offspring of the registration statement is the prospectus and is referred to variously by EDGAR as 424B1, 424B2, 424B3, and so on. This is what a securities holder receives to describe her rights.

Other Interesting Documents

Say what you will about the Securities and Exchange Commission, they do love their forms on F Street. (The document describing the forms themselves and how to properly file them clocks in at 125 pages!) In addition to the forms we reviewed here, an aggressive researcher intent on mastering business and corporate research at a professional level should learn some of the other popular forms, each of which is prescribed for a specific event in a corporation's life. See the complete rundown at the SEC's site by clicking on "Descriptions of SEC Forms." Listed here are some of the more interesting ones and what they do.

Form	Purpose
S-4/ F-4	Business combinations
13-D	Reports when an organization or individual acquires 5 percent of the company's outstanding shares
ARS	Annual report to shareholder, the fancy version of Form 10-K
S-8	Employee benefit plans
Sc T-O	Tender offer statement; a third-party is offering to buy large numbers of shares, not from the company but from current shareholders
13E-3	Going private transactions
14D-9	Tender offer solicitation
F-6	Registration of American depositary receipts
144A	Private placement; a sale of securities not to the public but to recognized institutional buyers like big Wall Street banks

Secondary Sources

Rifling through EDGAR documents is the best way to see the nittiest and grittiest details of a company's operations. But you need not ask forgiveness for taking shortcuts if, in the press of time or in the interest of expedience, you turn to some predigested resources from publishers who have done the digging for you. In truth, professional researchers use these sources all the time and refer to the SEC documents only when very specific questions come up or exact disclosure language needs to be found.

Google Finance

By scooping up news, data from the stock exchanges, stories from blogs, and disclosure from the websites of public companies, Google Finance offers at-a-glance information about public companies from around the globe. Search by company name or ticker symbol to see current and historical stock prices, links to public filings, and an interesting stock price graph that correlates news reports to stock movements. Google Finance combines as much publicly available information about a public company as a web page can hold.

> Google Finance offers at-a-glance information about public companies from around the globe.

Analytical Resources

For primary source materials, sift through a company's EDGAR documents to find the legally binding information that a company must disclose. If you want to know about a company but have no appetite to read through a company's filings, try consulting analytical sources, where the filings have been digested by trained professionals and explanations persuasively drafted by Wall Street analysts. Most well-stocked libraries keep up a subscription to Value Line, where you'll find one-page profiles of companies and predictions for its prospects in the stock market.

There are far fewer Wall Street brokerages now than there were before the Great Recession. Nevertheless, many of the remaining brokers still maintain a staff of stock analysts who publish lengthy reports that aim for objective analysis of a company's operations. The reports are sold for substantial subscription fees to investors first, but do make their way eventually to business information resellers like OneSource. Check with your library for analyst reports from OneSource, Freedonia, or Thomson Financial Investext. Subscription services from Moody's Investor Services, Fitch, and Standard & Poor's also can provide ratings and reports on companies and their debt securities. These are not services you're going to get for yourself for $1.99 on an iPad app. They are pricey services designed for consumption by institutions. Put them on your wish list for when you next chat with your librarian.

Private Companies

Public companies are the glamorous ones. Their comings and goings monopolize the press. They command headlines when they are involved in big-money mergers or bankruptcies or when they develop some blockbuster new product or service. But public companies aren't the only game in town. Throughout the United States, in fact, thousands of companies operate perfectly profitable and useful operations without ever having to disclose to the public the details of their operations the way publicly traded companies do. Because these companies do not sell securities to the public, they do not fall under the SEC's disclosure rules and so are aptly referred to as *private* companies.

**Remember that private does not
necessarily equal small.**

Remember that private does not necessarily equal small. Multibillion-dollar companies like Facebook, agribusiness titan Cargill, oil and gas giant Koch Industries, and accounting and advisory conglomerate PricewaterhouseCoopers were still privately owned as of November 2011. *Forbes* magazine happily lists the 400 and 500 largest private companies in their special annual issue, and the companies that rise to the top of the list are heavyweights indeed, with revenues in the hundreds of millions to the multibillions in sales per year. Private companies well outnumber public ones, since private companies include the local pizzeria and the mom-and-pop stationery store at the nearest strip mall as well as small- to medium-size companies that employ 15 to 5,000 people.

Unfortunately, digging up information on private companies presents challenges that don't happen when researching public entities. The main problem is the lack of any equivalent to the SEC's EDGAR system for private companies. In a nutshell, private companies don't have to disclose much information about their operations, so they don't. That doesn't mean you can't find out anything about them, but it takes more work than public company research, and what you can find is limited. The laborious part of private company research is cobbling together information from a variety of sources to get a clear portrait of the company. There is no one-stop shopping for private companies.

The laborious part of private company research is cobbling together information from a variety of sources to get a clear portrait of the company.

For private companies, the obvious first task is to see if the company maintains a website. If so, see what information you can glean from it: where the company operates, who owns the operation, what products the company makes, where it is located, and other tidbits that a company would voluntarily reveal about itself to the public.

The heavy lifting on private company research is best left to the professionals. A number of resources can offer the fruits of their own research (for a fee). Dun & Bradstreet and Hoovers are the two commercial publishers that provide information on privately held companies. Both of them sell their information to subscribers. For business researchers, Hoovers offers two plans: a subscription for researchers who do large-volume research and an on-demand type of account for the occasional researcher. Contact the companies for details on their prices. However, any well-equipped business library should provide access to these services, and the oft-repeated advice still holds: Check with the reference desk to see if they can run reports for you.

Every state secretary of state maintains a searchable database of companies that have registered to do business within the state.

Locate additional basic information by searching through the public records. Every state secretary of state maintains a searchable database of companies that have registered to do business within the state, which will provide at least the name of the company's owner, a headquarters address, and the name of the person who receives the legal papers for the company. Private companies operating in heavily regulated industries such as banking, insurance, or the energy sector will also be required to file reports with state and federal regulators; these reports are excellent sources for detailed information about these entities. Turn to the state departments that oversee these industries for annual reports or to the federal overseers, such as the National Information Center from the Federal Reserve (bank information), the National Association of Insurance Commissioners (insurance), or the Federal Energy Regulatory Commission (energy).

Your local library should also stock a few reference titles that won't overwhelm your information gathering senses but that will prove helpful in a pinch. *Ward's Business Directory of U.S. Private and Public Companies* and *Standard & Poor's Register* both list private companies, with some minimal indication of location and estimated gross annual sales. These lists are useful in finding businesses from a particular industry or to see who operates in a given location.

International Companies

As with research into private companies, international company searches hinge on services that harvest this information for a living. Again, a good business library should be able to provide you with access to these services or at least have them available to the research staff to consult on your behalf, since the subscription prices to them are designed for institutions, not individuals. OneSource is an excellent company profile service that offers snapshots of corporations worldwide. The service is not cheap, so check with your library and see if they subscribe. Other big players in the international company information hustle are Mergent Online (which restricts its coverage to publicly traded companies from around the globe) and Bureau van Dijk. Check your library too for services from Thomson Reuters, an immense business news operation. Best of all is a Bloomberg terminal. The Bloomberg, as most researchers call the dedicated computer, serves up an unending stream of business news and analysis and contains an information universe for virtually any company on planet Earth.

Some countries and their stock exchanges maintain disclosure systems similar to, but not as robust as, EDGAR. In Canada, SEDAR makes public annual reports and the like from Canadian issuers. For UK companies, the Financial Services Authority has a searchable database of company filings; you may also check the subscription-based Companies House or Perfect Information if you need in-depth access to UK filings. On the European continent, the bourses of Luxembourg, Paris, Frankfurt, and Rome offer limited information about companies listed on their exchanges, though you would do better to try OneSource or Perfect Information first. The same advice applies to Asian, Latin American, and emerging market companies. Secondary sources are better to consult than trying to get information from either the bourses or the local regulators.

Nonprofit Organizations

The vast majority of business organizations in the United States are created for the explicit purpose of making a profit. Charitable organizations, religious charities, secular do-gooders, and private foundations that dole out money to worthy causes, on the other hand, exist to provide a service, with no profit motive in mind. Most nonprofit organizations are known as 501(c)(3) corporations, from the section of the federal tax law that exempts their income from taxation. Because of that special status, they are collectively known as "exempts."

As part of their tax-exempt status, nonprofits are required by federal law to make their tax returns public. The annual Form 990 (Return of Organization Exempt from Income Tax) is the only tax return that is, as the IRS puts it, "open to public inspection." A Form 990 is the best source of information about a charitable organization. It looks like a standard tax form, with the expected "Subtract Line 42 from Line 36" instructions, but take a closer look: Inside, you'll find out how much money an organization took in and where it got it. Just as important, you'll learn what the charity actually does with the money: who got paid what to manage the operation and how much of the donated money was actually spent delivering whatever social good the 501(c)(3) said it provides. In short, Form 990 is the window into the operation of tax-exempt organizations. To get your hands on the form, check with the organization itself or, better, get it from GuideStar.

In short, Form 990 is the window into the operation of tax-exempt organizations.

IRS PUBLICATION OF 501(C)(3) CORPORATIONS

To find out if an organization qualifies as a 501(c)(3) company, check the IRS's database "Search for Charities." It's the online version of the venerable Publication 78, better known in print as *Cumulative List of Organizations Described in Section 170(c) of the Internal Revenue Code of 1986*. The database is quicker, easier, and better for your back muscles than trying to leaf through the heavyweight print volume.

The fittingly named GuideStar is the marquee name for charities research. If you don't want to spend your afternoons plucking factual tidbits from tax forms, turn instead to this website where the Guide-Star analysts have done a lot of the hunting, gathering, and analysis for you. This site not only provides the 990s from nonprofits but digests them into searchable reports on thousands of charities. The basic services are free, but if your research finds you sailing into the deeper waters of doing good, it could be worthwhile to invest in a premium account. The paid version of GuideStar expands on the basic information and allows for searching of very detailed data that are likely of greatest interest to charity professionals, lawyers, and curious reporters.

Research into a charity or its wealthier counterpart, the foundation, should also include a quick spin through the Foundation Center. It's a comprehensive database matching grant-making foundations with causes needing funding. The services of the center also include information on philanthropy in general and ideas about how to operate nonprofit activities most effectively. It's a good source for information on the world of charitable giving.

While it's unfortunate that some crooks run fraudulent charities, most states keep an eye on nonprofit organizations through their attorneys general's offices. They empower their head prosecutor to regulate charities within their state borders. Any research into suspect operations should include a call to the attorney general's office in the state where the charity operates. Precisely what information is made public varies from state to state, but most will make available whatever state filing is analogous to federal Form 990. In New York, for example, the attorney general's Charities Bureau publishes the annual registration statement for charities on a publicly available database, so it's easy to find information on tax-exempt operations within the state. These databases help the public make sure that charities do the good things they say they are doing.

Research Guides

This chapter's basic resources and search techniques will get you started, but as you discover that deeper digging into your subject is required, you'll need guidance on where else to look. Since researchers of all stripes, not just businesspeople, use corporate information, skill at looking up company info should be a basic tool in your reference repertoire. Luckily, many librarians worked overtime to publish guides just to help bewildered researchers find a path through the jungle of information. You can put your hands on most of the best

> **Skill at looking up company info should be a basic tool in your reference repertoire.**

research guides by consulting the meta-collection guides hosted by the University of North Texas. The UNT researchers looked at the major business libraries in the United States and linked to the research they found there.

I also recommend the online guide *Searching for Company Information* from the New York Public Library's Science, Industry, and Business Library. It's a gem of concise and thrifty advice for both novice and experienced business researchers alike. On a single web page, the librarians explain exactly which books you ought to be consulting for a variety of typical research requests into companies and industries: how to find minority-owned businesses or how to find companies active in a specific industry, for instance. If you're really interested in the subject, take the library's online class "Prospecting for Business Information." And, of course, always check in with your local library or nearest business library to see what they can offer. Chances are they will own the reference titles the NYPL recommends or can access them on your behalf.

Products Research

Corporate research doesn't always begin with a search into the particulars of a given company but rather with a specific product. Asking "Who makes this?" or "Who provides this type of service?" can lead directly to companies operating within a given industry. A couple of very fine and totally free services will help with the detective work needed to locate the companies behind certain products.

The Thomas Register began life as a set of very large and very green books. In its web incarnation, these books are available through ThomasNet (discussed in Chapter 5). Another service is the

Household Products Database from the National Library of Medicine, which makes it easy to find out who manufactures such standard consumer products as Comet, Windex, Formula 401, and 3-In-One multipurpose oil. To find makers of industrial products, turn to the "Industrial Quick Search Manufacturers Directory."

Industry Research

Companies operate within specific industries. Many a business research project begins not at the company level but higher up on the economic food chain, by gathering information about a specific industry. Industry research is a good way to get a handle on the environment in which a specific type of company operates. Whether you're tracking down trends in retailing, comparing the earning of steel manufacturing, or getting your arms around the latest trends in the cosmetics racket, industry research is good place to start.

Standard Industrial Classification Codes
Before setting out on any industry research, though, make sure you have a good grasp of the industrial classification codes. These codes are used to precisely describe a specific industry and to sort online databases by industry.

The two classifications systems that are most widely used are the Standard Industrial Classification Code (SIC) and the North American Industry Classification System (NAICS). The NAICS was developed to harmonize the classification systems of the United States with those of Mexico and Canada after the adoption of the North American Free Trade Agreement (NAFTA). You'll do just fine with the old-fashioned SIC code, which it is still widely used.

Because so many government agencies and commercial data services rely on these numbers to index information, you'll do yourself a great favor by understanding them. For example, if you want to gather a list of companies that manufacture aircraft, look up the SIC code for "aircraft," which is 3721. Now take that number and plug it in to the SEC's EDGAR company search database to generate a list of publicly traded companies in the airplane business. When I ran the SIC search, the result was a list of forty companies in the industry, including Boeing, Gulfstream Aerospace, and Embraer Brazilian Aviation Co. Other common uses of the SIC might be to see injuries reported to the Occupational Health and Safety Administration for this particular industry. Search the "Fatality and Catastrophe Investigation Summaries" and sort the data report by SIC. (Be forewarned that the injuries described in the report can be gruesome.) Or if you want to determine what pollutants various industries emit in selected locations, then the SIC is the number to use to pinpoint your data. Most industry reference books and many analytical reports use the number as well. It's well worth the time to look over the SIC system simply because it is a basic tool for filtering online information systems with precision and accuracy.

> It's well worth the time to look over the SIC system simply because it is a basic tool for filtering online information systems with precision and accuracy.

Associations

The value of associations as information sources was reviewed in detail in Chapter 6, so there is not much more add to the discussion other than to reinforce the idea that every industry has a professional association that will be glad to help you with research. They'll provide you with plenty of interesting data, or they'll point to you someone who can compile said pile of interesting data.

Directories

Even the most rudimentary search in your local library catalog should unearth a selection of directories, phone book–like listings of companies and industry sources from which to pick. The information contained in most of them is fairly bare bones and won't provide much more than a rundown of which companies operate in a selected industry. Use the lists as a starting point for research into the individual companies. As I mentioned before, the business directories most frequently found in the library are *Ward's Business Directory of U.S. Private and Public Companies* and the *Standard & Poor's Register Corporate*. In fact, for any type of industry directory, you should try one of the many titles available from Gale Cengage Learning, publishers of the venerable *Ward's Directory*. Gale has an impressive roster of directories for many leading industries, such as:

- *American Wholesalers and Distributors Directory*

- *Major Financial Institutions of the World*

- *Major Food and Drink Companies of the World*

- *Major Telecommunications Companies of the World*

From the same source that lists all of the directory titles, the tireless librarians at the New York Public's Science, Industry, and Business Library offer a list of directories for dozens of industries at a page quite naturally titled *Industry Specific Directories*. This is an excellent resource for locating reference materials, most of which should be available locally to you or by requesting it from a reference librarian.

Industry Magazines

Every industry has one or two periodicals covering the news. For a comprehensive listing of titles in specific sectors, the standard reference works are *Ulrich's Periodicals Directory* and *Directory of Business Information Resources*. It might also help to find a relevant association and then call them to ask what magazines or newspapers cover their business.

Industry-Specific Surveys and Rankings

The Fortune 500 is a household name. Each year, *Fortune* magazine ranks the top 500 American public companies. This list has become a badge of honor for any self-respecting corporation. In fact, it's become a shorthand way of referring to big, successful companies. Since the list first appeared, the Fortune 500 ranking has made the magazine a must-read and put the name of the magazine on the tongue of every business executive. Other publications have aped Fortune's formula and produce their own annual rankings. AmLaw100 is the ranking of the top U.S. law firms, from *American Lawyer* magazine. Other industry-specific lists are available, such as the Top 200 Catalog Companies, Top 100 Retreaders, and 20 Largest Electronic Recyclers. Many industry-specific magazines rank companies they cover. To find out what rankings are available and from which magazines, consult the Special Issues site, a list of lists, originally compiled by indefatigable librarian Gary Price. The free public database is out of date, but the lists can still serve as a handy guide to the names of rankings you might be interested in. And I'm sure that you won't be surprised to hear that the researchers from the NYPL's Science, Industry, and Business Library offer a lengthy list of industry surveys for your delectation.

SITES AND SOURCES MENTIONED IN THIS CHAPTER

Bloomberg
www.bloomberg.com

Bureau van Dijk
www.bvdinfo.com/Home.aspx

Census Bureau *NAIC/SIC Industrial Codes*
www.census.gov/eos/www/naics

Companies House
www.companieshouse.gov.uk

Dun & Bradstreet
www.dnb.com

Federal Energy Regulatory Commission
www.ferc.gov

Federal Reserve System, National Information Center
www.ffiec.gov/nicpubweb/nicweb/nichome.aspx

Financial Services Authority
www.fsa.gov.uk

Fitch Ratings
www.fitchratings.com/index_fitchratings.cfm

Foundation Center
www.foundationcenter.org

Freedonia
www.freedoniagroup.com

Google Finance
http://finance.google.com

GuideStar
www.guidestar.org

Hoovers
www.hoovers.com

Household Products Database
http://hpd.nlm.nih.gov

Industrial Quick Search Manufacturers Directory
www.industrialquicksearch.com

Industry Specific Directories
www.directory-pages.com/specific-directories.htm

Internal Revenue Service, Exempt Organizations Select Check
http://apps.irs.gov/app/eos

Mergent Online
www.mergentonline.com/login.php

Moody's Investor Services
www.moodys.com

National Association of Insurance Commissioners (NAIC)
www.naic.org

New York Attorney General's Charities Bureau Registry Search
http://bartlett.oag.state.ny.us/Char_Forms/search_charities.jsp

New York Public Library, Science, Industry, and Business Library, Industry Surveys
www.nypl.org/research/sibl/trade/surveys.html

New York Public Library, Science, Industry, and Business Library, Specific Industry Directories
www.nypl.org/research/sibl/trade/index.cfm

OneSource
www.onesource.com

Perfect Information
www.perfectinfo.com

Searching for Company Information (SIBL)
http://legacy.www.nypl.org/research/sibl/company/c2index.htm

Securities and Exchange Commission Descriptions of SEC Forms
www.sec.gov/info/edgar/forms/edgform.pdf

Securities and Exchange Commission, EDGAR
www.sec.gov/edgar/searchedgar/webusers.htm

SEDAR
www.sedar.com

Special Issues
www.specialissues.com/lol

Standard & Poor's
www.standardandpoors.com/home/en/us

ThomasNet
www.thomasnet.com

Thomson Financial Investext
http://research.thomsonib.com

Thomson Reuters
http://thomsonreuters.com

University of North Texas Libraries, Company and Industry Research
www.library.unt.edu/research-tools/guides/company-and-industry-research

U.S. Department of Labor, Occupational Safety and Health Administration, Fatality and Catastrophe Investigation Summaries
www.osha.gov/pls/imis/accidentsearch.html

Value Line
www.valueline.com

Wall Street Journal
www.wsj.com

Researching the Public Record

In the first season of the HBO series *The Wire*, most of the detectives investigating drug dealing in a Baltimore housing project spend their time tailing suspects, tapping phones, or roughing up the locals. But one veteran detective has a better idea—he decides to follow the money. He dispatches his detectives to look through tax assessment records for a nightclub where the kingpin's gang congregates. They're trying to find out whose name is listed on the tax records and then to head to the Maryland Corporate Charter office. It's there, he explains, that they should rifle through the paperwork on all corporations and limited liability companies licensed to do business in the state and write down every name they see. He wants to find out about any front companies owned by the drug dealers to hide their profits. The detectives will find those front companies by looking for the name of the registered agent who set up the companies on behalf of the kingpin. He wants to show how the drug proceeds end up in shell corporations and eventually the pockets of corrupt officials by looking for suspects in the file cabinets not by kicking in doors.

It's not every day you see such a concise illustration of public records research on a TV show, but there it was—the scriptwriters were making the dusty detective work of sifting records for useful facts almost as exciting as a street-level gunfight. Every private eye, every enterprising reporter, every diligent lawyer, and even TV detectives know one secret about looking up information: There is a treasure trove of factual information hiding in plain sight in documents and databases maintained by public agencies.

There is a treasure trove of factual information hiding in plain sight in documents and databases maintained by public agencies.

About Public Records

Public records are essentially the facts that various branches of government compile as they go about enforcing, interpreting, or creating the law. They're the documents and data we create by virtue of living in a society that needs to know something about us to function smoothly. As the name quite clearly says, public records are accessible to anyone who wants to see them. Unlike private records—contracts, bank accounts, tax returns, health records, and the like, which are the business of only the subject, authorized users, or litigation lawyers—public records belong to the people.

Inasmuch as public records are maintained by government agencies, you'll do well to remember where they are produced. So hark back to eighth-grade social studies and those memories of the three branches of government: the executive, the legislative, and the judicial. In the United States, both the federal government and the fifty state governments follow the same three-branch structure. The executive branch agencies are where the vast majority of the records you'll be interested in come from, because they enforce the laws the legislatures pass, though court and legislative sources can contain interesting data about people and companies as well.

At first blush, the idea of rooting around in bureaucratic files sounds about as exciting as cleaning out a closet. But just when the idea of running queries in databases starts to pall, I think about the rice pudding restaurant.

In a part of Little Italy in New York that transformed from a one-time Italian ghetto to the trendy and ultra-expensive, boutique-filled area now known as Nolita, is a restaurant that serves only rice pudding. Now, interesting restaurants can be found all over New York, but even by New York standards, it's hard to imagine that demand for rice pudding could be enough to sustain such a specialized operation. What was most unusual was the restaurant's location, on a now-gentrified stretch of Spring Street where high-end boutiques and celebrity-filled lounges have replaced clam bars and self-serve laundries that once dominated the street. Rents are astronomical.

A reporter friend of mine was curious about the pudding shop, so we decided to do a bit of sleuthing to find out more about the place. Our first move was to look up the owners of the building in which the store operated. In New York City, real estate records are available on a database called ACRIS, hosted by the city's Department of Finance. The address led us to the owner's name, in this instance a realty company. The name of the company didn't mean anything to us, so our next step was to see who the owner of the company was. The New York state secretary of state maintains a publicly available database of corporation and business records. We queried the database about the realty company and got the name of the principal owner. The name of the owner still didn't make sense, so that's when we decide to Google the owner's name. Among the list of results was a news story that mentioned the wife of a known mob boss, which also matched the name of the owner of the realty company.

Coincidence? Perhaps, but we decided to check it out by taking another dive through the ACRIS database, this time using the name of the realty company to see what other properties the company controlled. Within ten minutes, we had the answer. The company owned or controlled a number of buildings throughout Little Italy and NoLita. Another Google search on some of the addresses pulled up news stories about federal investigations into certain racketeering activities. By piecing together these ho-hum real estate records and corporation ownerships and combining them with Google searches for additional information, we discovered a possible explanation for why a rice pudding restaurant could make a go of it in the middle of the trendiest neighborhood in New York. A month or two later, the *New York Times* reported that the restaurant's owner and others were arrested and charged with operating a $21-million-a-year gambling operation out of the basement of the rice pudding building. (There was never any evidence that the restaurant was involved in any of the alleged operation, and ever since the case became public, the names in the records have been changed.) The point is, public records can tell stories that other sources can't.

Records come into existence in the course of ordinary business as a way to serve some important public policy goals. For example, one worthwhile goal is to make driving on the highway safer. One way states do that is by requiring those who want to use the highway to prove that they're competent drivers. They have to take a test and obtain a license. That's a sensible regulation. We share the public highways, and I need to know that you know how to drive. The entire real estate industry runs on the ability to check titles, liens, and ownership. The public benefits from knowing if a physician is licensed to practice medicine or if a pilot is qualified to fly a particular type of aircraft. You might like to know, too, if someone convicted of a sexual offense has moved into your neighborhood after release from custody or whether your bank is still in good standing with the bank examiner. Corporation and company records, business records of all types, permits, licenses . . . they're all part of the public record and are exactly the type of documents you need to consult to help you find out anything. As we'll see, they're collected by government agencies at all levels from behemoth federal cabinet departments right down to the rural county courthouse, and with just a few exceptions, they're ready for you to have for the asking.

Types of Public Records

Public records can be categorized into three neat pigeonholes: records that anyone can look at by walking in off the street (or searching online), records that are available for inspection by anyone who can prove a legal need to see them, and records that a public agency doesn't routinely make public but that must be disclosed when asked.

Records Available for Public Inspection

Documents or databases that are open to public inspection are the most public of public records. And we can be thankful that most of these records are "digitally born," making it much easier to obtain them. Back in the day when forms and filings were recorded on paper, a researcher had to trudge from one clerk's office to another, a process every bit as laborious as it sounds. E-records, though, can be quickly loaded up to a server for all but instant access. Plus, many agencies now are scanning their archival records to make items that were filed originally on paper readily accessible on the web.

Restricted Access

Certain records are maintained by public agencies but access to them is restricted to individuals or companies that can prove they have a legal interest in them. Likewise, access to vital records—birth certificates, death certificates, marriage licenses—is entirely restricted to those who have a legal right to them. Such individuals include the subject of the document, the next of kin, parents or legal guardians, executors of an estate and lawyers.

Records That Must Be Requested

Government agencies create documents or keep records of their work that are not routinely made available for public inspection. These materials can be provided to the public, but they are produced only when someone asks for them. In the event that an agency refuses to hand over the records, a citizen may file a Freedom of Information Act (FOIA) letter to formally request that the agency produce the information. We'll talk about the FOIA and its state equivalents later in this chapter.

Before we get into the details of public records research, look at the personal record you (hypothetically) already have left. You were born (birth certificate) and grew up somewhere (school records, phone number in the phone book). In your teenage years, you finally mastered parallel parking (driver's license), graduated high school (diploma), and registered to vote (voter registration rolls). You went to college (another diploma) and did a stint in the military (military records, discharge documents). You got married (marriage certificate) and bought a little house in the suburbs (mortgage lien). Maybe you learned how to fly a plane (pilot license). Imagine, then, after years of probity and rectitude, you decide to make a midlife career change to pursue the criminal arts.

Unfortunately, it turns out that you're a third-rate crook. You get arrested, arraigned, and tried (court proceedings, conviction record). The judge sentences you to a trip to jail (inmate locator records). That led to a loss of income (bankruptcy filing) and divorce (divorce decree). And awaiting your personal exit from this mortal coil is the ultimate document in your cradle-to-grave progression through this earthly life: the death certificate. In between, there are dozens of other documents, some public, many not, lying around government file cabinets throughout the country. Next time you can't sleep at night, don't count sheep. Instead, try to figure out where those customs forms you filled out on the plane coming back from spring break in Cancún now reside today.

Now think how interesting it would be to find out the details contained in those documents on a person or company. Mining these documents for the nuggets of information they hold is what public records research is all about. Inside these documents and computer records you'll likely find data on:

- Assets

- Addresses and phone numbers

- Company information

- Criminal records

- Licenses

- Prison inmates

- Property records

- Sexual offenders

- Voter registration

Every day credit agencies and marketing companies tap into this reservoir of information about people. They compile data on individuals to find out about where they live and what they own and make estimates of income based on Census Bureau data. The same sources they use are available to you. Public records research can provide insight about people and companies that can't be dredged up with a Google search.

Public records research can provide insight about people and companies that can't be dredged up with a Google search.

Yet there's a big *but* in records research. Billions of available records are held by thousands of agencies. As you can readily discern, there are lots of interesting records available for you to search. Getting to all of them is the problem. On one hand, researchers have a vast collection of information to consult; on the other hand, finding the right office, data collection, and record to search is a bearish problem simply because of the number of searchable offices and records.

Although I think self-sufficiency in information gathering is a great thing, you probably should not attempt your initial public records research by yourself. Instead, rely on the guidance of professionals, including websites that do the legwork for you and commercial sites that gather all this disparate information and roll it into a single, digestible package. Only with a good understanding of which records can be retrieved and where you can get them should you venture out into the wilds of the .gov domain. If you're up for the trek, query the index and request your documents from a public office—you will soon find yourself knee-deep in facts that you would have missed without looking into what the government knows and shares. Later in this chapter, I'll show you where to start with federal, state, and county searches to at least get you to the records trailhead. How far you go down the trail is entirely up to you. But in any event, get a solid grounding in the deep details of records searching with some instruction from the pros.

Finding Public Record Information

The Sourcebook

When I was a rookie, first starting out in research and couldn't tell a certificate of incorporation from a FOIA request, I was bewildered by the process of making sense of all the records available. There were too many agencies and too many records to think about. So I set out to figure out how to master the process. Much of what I know about public records research comes from *The Sourcebook to Public Record Information*, now in its tenth edition. Much as I would like to be your sole guide through the thickets of research, I will instead turn you over to the masters. Authors Peter Weber, Michael Sankey, and Peter J. Weber have compiled the standard work for public records research, and I cannot recommend this book enough. As do most experienced librarians and professional researchers, I still rely on it. It's an extremely detailed—more than 1,900 pages!—how-to guide for shaking the most fruit out of the bureaucratic tree. In light of the exhaustive treatment the authors give the topic, the overview of public records in this chapter should be considered merely an introduction. In addition to pointing to where the records are kept and describing what identifiers will help you locate specific records, the *Sourcebook* also takes you by the hand through the process of getting records from specific agencies and explains what you need to have in hand to get the right record. Your library probably has the book on the shelf, but if you find that the type of research you normally conduct requires public records retrieval, by all means, buy a copy of the *Sourcebook*. The website from its publisher BRB Publications gives away links to some free records and publishes a helpful tip of the day.

I'll also mention *Zimmerman's Research Guide*. Andrew Zimmerman is a law librarian who compiled a list of interesting websites for the benefit of his colleagues. His collection of links, which include many public records sources with brief annotations, is now a free service from Lexis and a worthy source of advice on where and how to look up a variety of public records.

Websites for Public Record Searches

Because thousands of county, state, and federal offices hold records of one type or another, your ability to harvest all that fruit bumps up against some practical limitations: Checking with each agency yourself takes forever. Luckily, you can save yourself hours of searching by using a content aggregator. Rather than having to query the 3,000+ county clerk offices or myriad state and federal agencies individually, these pay-for services have done the legwork for you electronically and amassed those records into one giant database. Avail yourself of the now-computerized records from filing clerks around the nation. If you could bring an old-school 1920s gumshoe back to life, he would be amazed at how easy it is to whip through millions of public records from the comfort of a computer chair. The services are not cheap, ranging in price from $19.99 up to $100 or more per search, depending on the amount of detail you need, but they do offer detailed information from public records conveniently and quickly.

Avail yourself of the now-computerized records from filing clerks around the nation.

Commercial Services

Intelius is a commercial service for people searches, background checks, and criminal records retrieval, with reports fashioned from sources nationwide. So too is KnowX, which will provide answers for background information within the limitations of the Fair Credit Reporting Act. (You must promise not to use the information for hiring or insurance decisions, or establishing credit.) NETR Online is a database of environmental filings, but it does double-duty as a general-interest public records database for company information.

If you work for an organization with access to LexisNexis or Westlaw, then you have a way to search public records elegantly and quickly. Lexis subscribers have access to Accurint and other people-finder records; Westlaw subscribers have a variety of databases for people finding, company information, and other public records. If you don't have access, see if your local librarian does.

Free Services

Some free sites assist in public records searches, in addition to BRB Publications. The Knight Digital Media Center provides a first-rate collection of public records tutorials that contain links to a variety of agencies. The Free Public Records Search Directory from Online Searches LLC is helpful for state agency searches. And Virtual Gumshoe has many links to free resources.

Searching on Your Own

If you do decide to try your hand at turning up records on your own, my hat is off to you for your courage. To aid you in this demanding quest, here is the 50,000-foot view of the sources that can deliver the goods. Consult each site for details on the type of records the agency holds, the scope of the holdings (for example, how far back records go electronically and what needs to be requested from the archives) and what you'll need to provide the agency with to find what you want.

Federal Records
Federal agencies, courts, and Congress have useful information but, by far, the records held by the executive agencies under the president are where the vast majority of interesting stuff will be found.

> The records held by the executive agencies
> under the president are where the vast
> majority of interesting stuff will be found.

Federal Agencies

Popular infomercial pitchman Matthew Lesko, who once was a late-night TV staple, worked himself up into a lather proclaiming how easy it is to get free government grant money. He might want to expand his cheerleading for government largesse into public records research. As a source for studies, official data, white papers, and expertise on an encyclopedic range of subjects, nothing compares to the U.S. government. At the risk of sounding as hyperbolic as the hyperthyroidal Mr. Lesko, the U.S. gives away priceless quantities of information. Every federal agency, within the limits of its legal marching orders to regulate one or more sectors of American society, opens up its doors to the information it's collected. As a researcher, commit to memory the web address for the U.S. government's information portal: www.usa.gov. Once you step through this doorway and see how much information the government produces, your life as a researcher will change forever.

Although records about people are primarily the province of state governments, the feds track everything from political donations by individuals (Federal Election Commission) to legal firearms manufacturing (Bureau of Alcohol, Tobacco, Firearms, and Explosives) to investment advisers (Securities and Exchange Commission).

Take a spin through the "A–Z List of Agencies." It shouldn't be too hard to find the right agency that might hold the records you want to see. Where could you find statistics on the number of late-flight arrivals into Dallas-Fort Worth for that article you're writing on vacation travel with kids? Try the Federal Aviation Administration (FAA). If you're the marketing director for a large hospital conglomerate and want to know about trends in gerontology, how about looking up reports from the Administration on Aging? Need to understand the pernicious effects of carbon tetrachloride, which was commonly used as a dry cleaning agent some years ago? The Agency for Toxic Substances and Disease Registry stands at the ready to tell you.

Name a subject and chances are good that a federal agency has something to say about it. The State Department will give you the rundown of the political situation in Timbuktu, while the Department of Energy tracks the price of gasoline in Newburyport, Massachusetts. While they're doing that, the Animal and Plant Inspection Service is fretting about the expansion of European larch canker in the United States, and the U.S. Geological Survey is watching its seismographs for earthquakes from coast to coast. The Centers for Disease Control and Prevention (CDC) looks for microbes in your body; NASA looks for them on Mars. The list goes on and on because the government requires all the people and companies it regulates to provide it with information, which you can then read. The .gov domain is home to an immense array of discrete bits of data that are available to the public as part of the government's function as protector of the citizenry.

The reason agencies gather all these data is that they help them carry out their regulatory duties. Why does the flight attendant tell you that your "tray tables must be secured in their upright position" before landing? Because the FAA requires them to say so. And where does the FAA get off telling people what to do? The administration was empowered by Congress to make all rules and regulations necessary to make air travel safe. Like most federal agencies, the FAA studies what needs to be regulated, proposes rules, publishes rules, lets the public comment on them, and then adopts the rules. Each agency publishes its proposed rules in the federal government's daily newspaper of rule making, the *Federal Register*; for a rule to have legal effect, the agency must subsequently publish the final rule there as well. All the rules that federal agencies write are compiled into the multivolume rule book, the *Code of Federal Regulations* (CFR). The CFR is arranged by title, and each title is broken down into parts as a way to make it somewhat easier to find things. (The studies and databases that agencies publish are how they share information they collect for the purpose of promulgating regulations.) The *Federal Register* and the CFR are available from the U.S. Government Printing Office's website, as well as from Regulations.gov.

In the case of the flight attendant's admonition about the tray tables, it's mandated by Advisory Circular 121-24C ("Passenger Safety Information Briefing and Briefing Cards"), which replaced Advisory Circular 121-24B (February 1, 1999). These advisories implement regulations from Title 14 CFR Parts 121 and 135, which set out the rules that pertain to air carrier operations in which flight attendants are present. That should ease your mind on your next bumpy descent into O'Hare.

The benefits of using the websites of the federal government as your personal research library are many. You've already paid for the information with your tax money, so take it, it's yours. The databases and reports are vetted by professionals and so can be considered reliable (or, at least, official). The federal government has invested in web technology, so the sites are easy to use and usually offer queryable databases, news, and in-depth research. But best of all is their focus on specific subjects. Federal websites opt for depth over breadth. Deep diving into environmental data at the Environmental Protection Agency (EPA) is deep indeed.

You'll be doing yourself a great service if you spend an afternoon clicking through the different links from www.usa.gov. Answers to many a research question can be found from the right federal agency. Let the site be your guide to your (information) rich Uncle Sam.

Federal Courts

Most federal research is aimed at shopping the storehouses of information from the executive branch agencies and offices. But court filings are also useful sources of some juicy data. In these public filings are details of disputes that name names, cite information about private finances, and detail the conduct that resulted in a lawsuit. For a lawyer to prevail over an opponent, the rules of civil procedure require that an attorney provide detailed and verifiable facts to the court. Because court records are public documents (with the exception of certain cases involving minors, national security, or trade secrets and other sensitive topics), you can help yourself to this information as well. In court records you'll also find other goodies like real estate data, bankruptcy information, and allegations of bad doings by people and companies, backed up with facts and reports.

Your entry point to federal court documents is PACER (Public Access to Court Electronic Records), a subscription service for retrieving the dockets and documents for federal cases filed in district, appellate, and bankruptcy courts. Both individuals and companies may obtain subscriptions. PACER charges a very modest fee for downloading documents. Access to court documents costs 8¢ per page, though it may be raised to 10¢ in 2012. The cost to access a single document is capped at $2.40, the equivalent of thirty pages under the 8¢ pricing. The cap does not apply to name searches, reports that are not case specific, or transcripts of federal court proceedings. Instructions on how to use PACER can be found on its website.

The docket is the comprehensive list of documents filed with the court during a trial. When a case commences in court, it is assigned a docket number, and from then on, all papers, motions, and other documents submitted to court in the case are filed on the docket under that number.

The docket number is the unique identifier for each case and thus is critical to federal case research.

The docket number is the unique identifier for each case and thus is critical to federal case research. Generally, the docket number looks like this: *02 civ 0897 (JGM)*. Translated, this would be the docket number for a case that commenced in 2002, is a civil case, and is the 897th case opened in the court that year. The initials in parenthesis refer to the judge to whom the case was assigned.

The federal court systems grapple with issues of federal law. Individuals and corporations make federal cases out of copyright infringement, civil rights complaints, bankruptcy, violations of antitrust trust law, securities law, and other matters of U.S. law.

Federal Legislation

Making laws is proverbially an ugly business, but in a civil society ruled by law, not by individuals, it's a necessity. Modern technology hasn't made the process any less unsettling, but at least it's easier to lay your hands on proposed and adopted legislation.

To see what Congress is doing to move us closer to that more perfect union, consult Thomas, the legislative server at the Library of Congress. Thomas, named for President Jefferson, is a searchable database that simplifies the process of retrieving new laws or laws under consideration, known as bills.

The process of enacting legislation is complex; should you need a primer on how to look at the guides at Thomas itself, read "What You

Can Find on Thomas" to get a better orientation than the School-house Rock version provides. And now, in some very broad, oversim-plified strokes, here's how laws are made:

A bill is introduced into the House or Senate, where it is sent to the appropriate committee for review. The bill is given the third degree by a subcommittee; fully 90 percent of bills die here, never to be heard from again. But if there is political appetite and will to move the legis-lation, the bill is reported out of committee and debated and voted on by the chamber that introduced it. If it passes, it is now known as an engrossed bill and is sent to the other chamber, where the process starts all over again. If the other chamber approves it, the bill now is known as an enrolled bill and is sent to the president to be signed into law or vetoed. If the president approves the bill, it becomes a public law and is added to body of the federal law, collectively known as the U.S. Code.

At Thomas, you can tune in to bills at any step in the process. Thomas should also earn the gratitude of every nonlawyer for provid-ing plain-English explanations of what each of the bills is intended to do and for explaining exactly where the bill stands in its life cycle between introduction and presidential approval. Should you need to dig through pending legislation, don't just dive in; legislative research is a specialty of law librarians and it takes some special training to learn the lingo. Ask for help from a reference librarian, preferably a law librarian, to navigate this excellent but complicated compilation of federal lawmaking.

State Records

Using my state college math skills, I multiplied fifty states by twenty-five agencies and discovered that the product totaled up to . . . too many links to print here. Rather than inundate you with an indigest-ible laundry list of URLs to all the state agencies and their corresponding databases of public records, I'll give you a strategy to keep things simple.

Every state agency has a national association for the benefit of the administrators. That association, in turn, can do the laborious work of providing links to the office in each state. Not only will you get the URLs you need, you'll enjoy the added benefit of the association's explanations of what the state agencies do.

By looking at the associations for the state agencies, you'll also learn what types of records you might find on any given site. The banking administrators for each state, for example, generally provide a list of the institutions they regulate. You'll probably find a survey of bank data: who is solvent and who might not be, how institutions are meeting their community reinvestment obligations, and which banks may be in trouble.

The information resources from state agencies vary considerably from state to state. (The management of herds of buffalo and wild horses is not a state regulatory problem as urgent in New Jersey as it is in Montana.) But even with obvious state differences, the regulations and data required to govern are essentially the same from one jurisdiction to another. Every state will have an executive agency, under the control of the governor, to oversee and regulate certain industries as well as to provide fundamental services to citizens and companies within the state's borders. In every state, however, you may count on certain agencies to offer records about the companies and people who fall within their purview. Let's take a look at some of them.

Banking

In every state, an agency exists to set up and regulate state-chartered banks. (Note that banks may also be federally chartered.) You should be able to find, at minimum, the names of the banks that fall under the state's purview. In addition to information on banks, states usually regulate non-bank financial service companies, like check-cashing emporia. If the state is liberal with the information it publishes, you might be able to also see

- Banking regulations

- Enforcement actions against misbehaving institutions

- Licenses and bank charters

- Consumer information

Insurance

The insurance business is also regulated at the state level. The complexities of insurance law and regulations are too knotty to summarize here, so rather than try to explain the differences among states, I entrust you to the website of the National Association of Insurance Commissioners. What I can tell you is that insurance companies are domiciled in a certain state and then must be licensed to operate in other ones. The best guide for information on individual insurance companies is the multivolume set *A.M. Best Insurance Reports*. It's also available online, but at a subscription price designed for institutional subscribers. Your library might get the online version in addition to the books. Look to the state department of insurance website for particular regulations and insurance laws.

Motor Vehicles

Since the passage of the federal Drivers Privacy Protection Act, states now must follow standard guidelines that limit access to driver's license information. Rather than a state-by-state hodgepodge of laws, with some states giving away license data for the asking and others putting the information under serious access control, the federal law set one standard for natural materials, which said only agencies and businesses with a need to know may obtain the records. Check with the state in question for the regulations governing access, as there may be considerable differences among the rules of different jurisdictions.

Secretary of State (Corporations and Business Entities)

While the U.S. secretary of state flies around the globe negotiating treaties and attending international conferences as the nation's chief diplomat, state secretaries of state tend to lead much less glamorous lives. They certify election results and, in most states, oversee business and corporation records. The work may be humdrum, but in many ways the records that the secretary of state collects and manages are some of the most useful of all to the business researcher.

> **In many ways the records that the secretary of state collects and manages are some of the most useful of all to the business researcher.**

Of the primary duties of a secretary of state at the state level, the election certification process has the most political consequence—does Florida on election night 2000 ring a bell?—but certifying the results of elections is mostly a ministerial function. For the researcher, the real pot of information gold under the secretary's care are the business filings. Use business corporation searches to find the names of owners and addresses of principal places of business for all companies operating within a state's borders. Please note that a company does not need to be incorporated in a state to operate there. Many corporations trace their legal birth to Delaware, where the laws and courts are management friendly, but live out their business lives elsewhere. (A Delaware corporation operating in Albany, New York, is considered to be a "foreign corporation.")

Like the federal executive agencies, state executive agencies provide the lion's share of useful data. Each state's home page will serve as the portal to that state's agencies and their databases. And as courtesy to the states, long united, the federal portal www.usa.gov links to all of the state government home pages.

State Department and Primary Area of Responsibility	Links to State Agencies, Officials, or Administers Can Be Found at . . .
Agriculture	National Association of State Departments of Agriculture: www.nasda.org
Attorney general	National Association of Attorneys General: www.naag.org
Alcoholic beverages	National Conference of State Liquor Administrators: www.ncsla.org
Banking and financial institutions	Conference of State Bank Supervisors: www.csbs.org/Pages/default.aspx
Budget	National Association of State Budget Officers: www.nasbo.org
Corporations	National Association of Secretaries of State: www.nass.org
Corrections	Association of State Correctional Administrators: www.asca.net

State Department and Primary Area of Responsibility	Links to State Agencies, Officials, or Administers Can Be Found at . . .
Court administration	National Center for State Courts: www.ncsc.org
Education	Council of Chief State School: Officers www.ccsso.org
Environment	Environmental Council of the States: www.ecos.org
Governor	National Governors Association: www.nga.org/cms/home.html
Health	National Association of County and City Health Officials: www .naccho.org/membership/saccho/ map.cfm
Housing	National Council of State Housing Agencies: www.ncsha.org
Insurance	National Association of Insurance Commissioners: www.naic.org
Labor	Interstate Labor Standards Association: www.ilsa.net
Medicaid	National Association of State Medicaid Directors: www.nasmd .org/Home/home_news.asp
Motor vehicles	American Association of Motor Vehicle Administrators: www .aamva.org
Parks	National Association of State Park Directors: www.naspd.org

State Department and Primary Area of Responsibility	Links to State Agencies, Officials, or Administers Can Be Found at . . .
Parole	American Probation and Parole Association: www.appa-net.org/eweb
Police	American Association of State Troopers: www.statetroopers.org
Power	National Association of State Energy Officials: www.naseo.org
State	National Association of Secretaries of State: www.nass.org
State university	American Association of State Colleges and Universities: www.aascu.org
Taxation, revenue, and finance	Federation of Tax Administrators: www.taxadmin.org
Technology	National Association of State Technology Directors: www.nastd.org
Transportation	American Association of State Highway and Transportation Officials: www.transportation.org
Workers compensation	International Association of Industrial Accident Boards and Commissions: www.iaiabc.org

State Courts

For quick access to the websites of courts in each of the states, refer to the list maintained by the National Center for State Courts (NCSC). Not only will its website link you to state sites but the center had enough foresight to include a guide to each court's structure to show how litigation matters flow through the courts. Court hierarchy can be confusing to the nonlawyer and downright baffling to the novice. Case in point: Try to explain why it is that in New York, the lowest court is known as the Supreme Court and the highest court is the Court of Appeals. And where does a litigant bring the initial appeal from the Supreme Court? To the Court of Appeals, right? No, it goes to the Appellate Division first. I don't report this to confuse you but only to toughen you up for the court research ahead.

State courts are where the grittiest legal action takes place. While federal courts listen to disputes about bankruptcy, securities fraud, and tax matters, state courts hear cases about homicides, narcotics, arson, and other criminal matters. (They also hear slip-and-fall cases and routine commercial disputes in civil court.) Because each state's court system is unique in how it hears evidence in trial courts and structures the appeals process, consult your state's court administration site for guidance. NCSC provides all the links you'll need.

Among the records available through the clerk of the court are dispositions of criminal and civil matters and, in those instances in which a judge writes a decision in a case, a copy of the opinion. (Decisions are formally collected in a series of books known as "case reporters" and can be found in your county law library—most counties have one.) To obtain court records, you'll need to know at least the name of the party or parties in the case and preferably the docket number of the action. You also should know the court in which the case was being heard and, ideally, the name of the judge to which it was assigned. The website for the clerk of the court will detail the particulars needed to retrieve case information.

> To obtain any court records, you'll need
> to know at least the name of the party or
> parties in the case and preferably the docket
> number of the action.

State Legislative Information

With the exception of the unicameral Nebraska legislature, state lawmaking closely mirrors the federal process. There is a senate and an assembly, and the two chambers at the state level mimic the Washington, DC, pas de deux right down to the hearings, transcripts, and ultimate delivery of an enrolled bill to the governor for signing into law. For links to state houses, the excellent services of the National Conference of State Legislatures has the lowdown of what is going on legislatively among the fifty states. Each state maintains an official state library or even a state law library as a repository of its legislative histories, featuring bill texts, committee reports where available, and the final version of bills signed into law by the governor.

By looking at the bills, you can track state lawmaking to see what legislators are thinking about particular topics. But more important, committee reports accompanying the bill are a great source of insight into the reasoning lawmakers used to come up with their legal language. Lawyers call it legislative intent. Not all bills at the state level have them, but for those that do, the reports will clue you in to what lawmakers were trying to achieve when they wrote the law the way they did.

Administrative Rule Making

Like their federal counterparts, state executive agencies are given power by the legislature to promulgate regulations to enforce their little part of the law. Rules are drafted, published in the state version of the *Federal Register,* and then published again once the final rules have been adopted. The collection of state rules is known as the administrative code (which should not be confused with the laws of the state, the statutes). To see what an agency says about a particular topic, consult the appropriate admin code. Links to state codes are available as a courtesy to members of the National Association of Secretaries of State; membership is free, so sign up!

UCC Filings

The Uniform Commercial Code, known universally as the UCC, is a model law governing the day-to-day business transactions. Since the fundamentals of buying and selling, leasing, writing checks, selling things in bulk, and issuing investment securities are the same in Maryland and Nebraska, one set of laws serves many states (tailored by each state legislature to serve local needs). The UCC was drafted by an august group of legal scholars from the American Law Institute and the National Conference of Commissioners on Uniform State Laws and is used throughout the nation.

County Records

According to the National Association of Counties, the go-to source for all things county related, there are 3,068 counties in the United States. And every one of them employs a clerk to receive, file, and retrieve a variety of records. A county may be the smallest governmental unit to concern itself with detailed record keeping, but county clerk's offices are where some of the most informative filings are located. They are rich hunting grounds for factual information, particularly liens and real estate records.

> County clerk's offices are rich
> hunting grounds for factual information,
> particularly liens and real
> estate records.

Liens

A lien is a claim on property that exists until a debt is repaid. For liens to be useful, they have to declare to the world that they exist, which is why they are standard fare at most county clerk offices. Liens come in many varieties, but what they all represent is evidence of a loan. Among the most common types of liens are the following:

- **Mechanic's lien:** Contractors or subcontractors working on a property file these to protect their right to get paid, since they can't unhammer the nails or unplumb the pipes in cases of non-payment. These types of liens are also known variously as construction liens, suppliers' liens, or architects' liens, but the intent is the same.

- **Tax lien:** Tax authorities may place a lien on a property for non-payment of taxes.

- **Attorney's lien:** The barrister insures his fee.

- **Judgment lien:** This satisfies a legal judgment after a court ruling.

- **Maritime lien:** Liens may be filed against a ship for sailors' wages, pollution claims, and other issues arising from a ship's operation.

Liens are filed on a form known as UCC-1, which is created by the Uniform Commercial Code.

Real Estate Records

Of all the records to be found in county or municipal files, none is more interesting than the seemingly humdrum real estate record. Not merely a legal warehouse of prices paid and deeds transferred, real estate records can also document a person's wealth, change of ownership, and prices paid for specific properties; you'll be able to find deeds and tax documents. In short, use the county clerk's office as your personal information bank for locating assets, values of buildings and homes, and as a guide to who owns it all.

Working with Public Records

Searching with New Search Technology

The most significant development of the next evolution of the Internet is known as Web 3.0, or the "semantic Web." Search engines don't simply retrieve neat rows of numbers or deliver documents in response to queries; they also analyze the raw data to come up with more meaningful answers than simple data retrieval alone can provide. To exploit this new technology, Data.gov collects info from around the federal government and applies some interesting algorithmic magic to it. The public records it mines aren't ones about people or businesses specifically but instead are immense collections of scientific and commercial data: state education profiles, for instance, or refinery utilization or demographic data. The site itself encourages private developers to create apps or mash-ups with the data. It launched in 2009, so Data.gov is still in its infancy. To catch a glimpse of how data will be organized and analyzed in the future, see what Data.gov is doing today.

The much lauded Wolfram|Alpha is another computational search engine that digests sets of public data and produces interesting results by finding new patterns and insights from the materials it analyzes. The search engine can deliver socioeconomic data, information on people and history, scientific data, and medical information. If you're new to it, don't miss the online tutorials that explain just what Wolfram|Alpha is doing.

Freedom of Information Laws

One of the delights of living in a democracy is being able to demand information from the government, thanks to laws guaranteeing citizen access to government records. Since the passage of the Federal Freedom of Information Act (FOIA) in 1966, government agencies as disparate as the FBI and the Department of Energy have established offices specifically to handle requests for agency information, as FOIA requires. As the National Security Archive website puts it, FOIA "establishes the public's right to obtain information from federal government agencies." It also puts the burden on the government to explain why a record should not be made public.

As mentioned before, lots of public records are readily available. Many government agencies, though, release some of their information only upon request. Generally speaking, this tends not to be routine data, but instead are records that don't fit into a nice, neat bucket.

The National Security Archive has a thorough guide to FOIA, including background, the legislative history of the act, and how-to guides for filing FOIA requests. Researchers faced with obdurate agencies will learn how to wrest information from the hands of grabby bureaucrats with the detailed guides provided by the Reporters' Committee for Freedom of the Press. In addition to handy explanations to show you the ropes for government research, the site features an automated "FOIA Letter Generator": Plug in what you want to get and the FOIA Letter Generator will produce a post office–ready letter in minutes.

Also standing by to lead us through the ins and outs of the FOIA process is the Department of Justice. Its site explains the legal underpinnings of what FOIA can and cannot provide to the resourceful researcher. For all the weight that FOIA puts on government agencies to disclose information to the public, certain types of records remain exempt from the law's requirements. Not only can you *not* use FOIA to ask for the nuclear launch codes or the combination to the safe at Fort Knox, but there are nine other categories of information that agencies are under no obligation to disclose. The Reporters' Committee lists the exemptions and expands on how agencies use these exemptions to wriggle out of producing things the agency is obligated to disclose. FOIA specifically protects records that concern the following:

- Classified matters of national defense or foreign policy

- Internal personnel rules and practices

- Information specifically exempted by other statutes

- Trade secrets and commercial or financial information

- Privileged interagency or intra-agency memoranda or letters

- Personal information affecting an individual's privacy

- Investigatory records compiled for law enforcement purposes

- Records of financial institutions

- Geographical and geophysical information concerning wells

Other exemptions extend to records of law enforcement agencies and are models of common sense. They relieve law enforcement agencies from having to disclose even the existence of records for an ongoing investigation; records that would reveal the identity of confidential informants; those which, if made public, would deprive a person from a fair and impartial trial; ones containing personal information whose disclosure would constitute an unwarranted invasion of privacy; and information that would interfere with enforcement proceedings. In short, any request that would negatively affect police or law enforcement operation is disallowed under the FOIA rule.

But even working within the limitations of the rules, the FOIA legally obligates government officials to the spirit of openness in the conduct of public affairs. The almost natural reaction of most public officials is to be secretive. Prying loose what is, after all, information that belongs to the citizenry is good policy. When you come across a federal agency that obstinately refuses to turn over reports or data or other materials that are not otherwise specifically protected, the Freedom of Information Act puts a powerful tool in your hands to compel the officials to comply.

State FOI Rules

All states have freedom of information laws analogous to the federal law. The intricacies of the state rules, as well as the various ways that state agencies can be queried, are significant. Before you dive in to

> **Know the correct procedure for requesting
> the records you want to see because agencies
> are well within their rights to refuse
> requests that don't follow the game plan.**

the challenging world of state FOI requests, brush up on the precise details of what you may or may not obtain from a particular state. Know the correct procedure for requesting the records you want to see because agencies are well within their rights to refuse requests that don't follow the game plan. The most valuable guide to state agency FOI searching comes from the Reporters Committee. The committee publishes the *Federal Open Government Guide* and offers an invaluable state-by-state analysis. It evaluates and compares each state's regulations and policies on a table. Use the pulldown menu on its website to select the FOI policy and then choose the states whose laws on the matter you need to compare. This is very helpful when your search for records crosses state lines and you're not clear about what the policy is in different jurisdictions. By the way, the committee is a nonprofit organization and provides the guides pro bono. Making a donation in gratitude would not be a bad thing.

Public records research is like a treasure hunt.

Public records research is like a treasure hunt. By going from one agency to another with your list of needed information in hand, you will secure item after item until you've collected all the facts you need. The search can be tedious at times, but the breadth of information available to researchers today and the ease with which it can be gathered takes a lot of the sting out of the process.

For a vivid explanation of how an experienced reporter uses the public record to his best advantage, see *New York Times* journalist Mike McIntire's how-I-did-it story about tracking down the parties responsible for an otherwise anonymous political ad. In "The Secret Sponsors," McIntire illustrates the process of online research, which today constitutes the electronic equivalent of following the famous paper trail beloved by investigative reporters past. By poking around websites, sifting through corporate records, looking up Federal Election Commission filings, and checking other publicly available sources, enterprising reporters dig up facts. Reporters, like lawyers, librarians, and historians, appreciate the value of all the interesting facts that hibernate in file drawers and computer servers in clerks' offices around the nation.

TRY THIS AT HOME

Tapping into the vast repositories of the public record is one of the basic skills that all researchers should master. It is hard to overstate the value of being able to get at the billions of bits of data held by public agencies at every level of government. To drive home the value of knowing how to use the public record, use these exercises to pull up information about your neighborhood from these ten expansive databases.

I selected these databases to show the breadth of information that anyone can access. They are merely representative samples of federal databases; there are literally thousands of searchable databases published by the government. It would be challenging indeed to catalog all federal databases and describe what you might find lurking inside of them. And who'd read it? You've got www.usa.gov as your index to agencies already at your fingertips. The following ten questions will require you to query databases large and small and should illustrate what is going on in your own backyard.

Once you can see what information you can pull up quickly, I trust you'll see my point clearly: Agencies and their record collections have information that Google can't access. You, however, can scoop it up yourself—and quickly, at that—with curiosity and imagination as your principle research tools.

1. *Are the banks in my town financially sound?*

First thing to do . . . locate the banks in your town. The Federal Deposit Insurance Corporation maintains the "Bank Find" database that will do just that. Type in your zip code to generate a list of local banks. You'll see that each bank's name is linked to a report that, in turn, links to a number of fact-rich sites containing additional information, including the CALL/TFR financial information report. This report, from the Federal Financial Institutions Examination Council, contains income statements, demographic information, and just about any other piece of factual bank data that you may need to see.

2. *Who owns that truck going past my house? Does that trucking company hire safe drivers?*

States require trucks to display either their Department of Transportation identification number (U.S. DOT number) or motor carrier number (MC number) on the door of the vehicle. Next time you're walking down the street or driving in your neighborhood, jot down the DOT number of an area truck. Next, take a look at the SafeStat Online from the Federal Motor Carrier Safety Administration. Plug in the DOT number to generate a report on the carrier's safety record.

3. *How clean is the air in my town? Are local businesses allowed to handle hazardous waste? Can they emit pollutants into the air? What about toxic releases?*

The EPA collects vast amounts of data from businesses throughout out the nation. (Because of the agency's ardor for gathering data,

233

the EPA is always on the short list of government operations that antiregulation zealots would like to eradicate.) What do they have to report about environmental issues in your town? To get a comprehensive report on the air and water, and other information, merely type your zip code into the search box labeled "MyEnvironment" on the EPA's home page.

4. *What is the crime rate near me? How many robberies? Assaults?* Although the federal data sets don't get down to the town or zip code reporting levels that most other government databases do, you can still get some detailed reports for your state or, if you live in a city or town with a population over 250,000, of your metropolitan area. The Bureau of Justice Statistics has an extensive collection of searchable databases that illustrates the state of the criminal union. Take your pick—homicides, juvenile delinquents, crime trends—and start your statistical sleuthing. To really localize your results, find your local police precinct and see if it publishes crime data about your neighborhood.

5. *How many people over the age of sixty-five live near me? How many people have college degrees? What is the median income in my town?*
The Census Bureau cheerily slices and dices census information in dozens of interesting ways. The bureau's number crunchers tot up the results in a "FactSheet," a detailed statistical rundown of your zip code that compares a locality's statistics to national averages. Included in the report are numbers on general characteristics of the population such as age, gender, and household population as well as on ethnicity, education status, military status, and median income.

6. *What chemicals are in my kitchen cleaner? What exactly am I washing my clothes with? Are the ingredients in my car wax carcinogenic?*

In 1981, Lily Tomlin starred in a movie titled *The Incredible Shrinking Woman*. The comic plot was perfectly simple: Tomlin plays a conscientious housewife whose household cleansers, perfumes, and other products expose her to a laboratory's worth of chemicals as she keeps her house spic and span. Those chemicals reduce Tomlin to the size of a Barbie doll. Too bad she didn't have the Internet back then. She could easily have found out what mysterious compounds were under her kitchen sink or hiding in the garage by perusing the Household Products Database (which I also touted as a great source for company information—a good database serves many masters). The National Library of Medicine publishes the database, giving the public a field guide to the remarkable number of chemicals common in the home and workplace.

Try this. Walk around your house and pick up five things you use to clean, shine, polish, or scrub. Then find out what's contained in those products and the health effects of ingesting any of the constituent parts. Not only does this database report on the chemical makeup of thousands of products, it reports on the companies who manufacture them. It also can point you to the Material Safety Data Sheet, which is a scientific profile of the chemicals in the most ordinary of products. Did you know that the now-discontinued Febreze Laundry Odor Eliminator contained . . . hydrochloric acid?

7. *Who gives money to my congresswoman? Or my senator?*

Although Watergate mystery man "Deep Throat" never actually told the reporters Woodward and Bernstein to "follow the money"—that bit of memorable dialogue was the handiwork of

All the President's Men screenwriter William Goldman—the advice is still valid. Money talks, and when it does, no one cocks an ear more attentively than a politician. Take a look at who is doling out the allowances to your elected federal representatives at the Federal Election Commission's disclosure databases, where you can search contributions by candidate, individual donor, and committee donor and find a summary of political action committee/candidate contributions.

8. *Is my town at risk for a drought or flood? What about an earthquake? Are there valuable minerals beneath my land? Is the water safe to drink?*

The job of mapping the entire United States falls to the U.S. Geological Survey (USGS). Its interest in the underground scene also includes monitoring climate change, water tables, and land use. The USGS relies on something called geospatial analysis, which is a way to track how land is used. Use the state-by-state map to look up the geological and geographic facts about your local region.

9. *How expensive is it to live where I do?*

Keeping tabs on the cost of living is the job of the Bureau of Labor Statistics (BLS), which publishes a timely variety of databases and tables to track the rise and fall of prices for the stuff that everybody buys. The BLS calculates the well-known Consumer Price Index (CPI), a benchmark for many contracts, agreements, and government programs that depend on cost-of-living adjustments. Use the various charts and graphs from the BLS website to see how your metropolitan area fares on the spectrum of expensive to affordable areas to live.

10. *Are the schools in my neighborhood performing as well as they should be?*

The breadth and complexity of data on schools available from the Department of Education's National Center for Education Statistics are extraordinary. Dozens of charts, databases, and tables containing statistics and studies will present a clear picture of how schools in different districts are performing. Click through the "Fast Facts, Tables and Figures," and the "Data Tools" to dig up whatever piece of the educational puzzle you choose to explore.

SITE AND SOURCES MENTIONED IN THIS CHAPTER

Administration on Aging

www.aoa.gov

Agency for Toxic Substances and Disease Registry

www.atsdr.cdc.gov

Animal and Plant Inspection Service

www.aphis.usda.gov

Bank Find

www2.fdic.gov/idasp/main.asp

BRB Publications

www.brbpub.com

Bureau of Labor Statistics Consumer Price Index

www.bls.gov/cpi/#tables

Bureau of Justice Statistics
http://bjs.ojp.usdoj.gov/index.cfm

Centers for Disease Control and Prevention
www.cdc.gov

Code of Federal Regulations
www.gpo.gov/fdsys/browse/collectionCfr.action?collectionCode=CFR

Data.gov
www.data.gov

Department of Justice FOIA Guide
www.justice.gov/oip/foia_guide09.htm

Environmental Protection Agency
www.epa.gov

FactSheet
http://factfinder2.census.gov/faces/nav/jsf/pages/index.xhtml

Federal Aviation Administration
www.faa.gov

Federal Election Commission Disclosure Data Search
www.fec.gov/finance/disclosure/disclosure_data_search.shtml

Federal Register
www.gpo.gov/fdsys/browse/collection.action?collectionCode=FR

FOIA guidance
www.rcfp.org/foia

FOIA Letter Generator from the Reporter's Committee for Freedom of the Press
www.rcfp.org/foia

Free Public Records Search Directory
http://publicrecords.onlinesearches.com

Household Products Database Health and Safety Information on Household Products
http://householdproducts.nlm.nih.gov

Intelius
www.intelius.com

Knight Digital Media Center
http://multimedia.journalism.berkeley.edu/tutorials/cat/public-records

KnowX
www.knowx.com

Lexis/Nexis
http://lexisnexis.com

Library of Congress, Thomas
http://thomas.loc.gov

NASA
www.nasa.gov

National Association of Counties
www.naco.org

NETR Online
www.netronline.com

National Center for Education Statistics Fast Facts, Tables and Figures, Data Tools
http://nces.ed.gov

National Security Archive
www.gwu.edu/~nsarchiv

Open Government Guide
www.rcfp.org/ogg

PACER
www.pacer.gov

Safe Stat Online
http://ai.fmcsa.dot.gov/SafeStat/SafeStatMain.asp?PageN=results

"The Secret Sponsors"
www.nytimes.com/2010/10/03/weekinreview/03mcintire.html?_r=1&
ref=weekinreview

Sourcebook to Public Record Information
www.brbpublications.com/books/details.asp?ProductID=515

U.S. Geological Survey
www.usgs.gov/state

U.S. Government Portal
www.usa.gov

Virtual Gumshoe
www.virtualgumshoe.com/index.asp

Westlaw
www.westlaw.com

Wolfram|Alpha
www.wolframalpha.com

Zimmerman's Research Guide
http://law.lexisnexis.com/infopro/zimmermans

10

Putting It All Together

Few things are truly hidden anymore. It was romantic once to know about something that no else did, like a rare jazz record or an undiscovered gem of a book. The days of obscurity are over. Thanks to Google, the databases of the deep web, online research materials, electronic books, and the knowledge stored in the minds of smart people with whom we can talk, even the most arcane fact is waiting in the open for us.

===================================
**The process of finding things out
means making connections.**
===================================

Regardless of what new wonders technology may bring us next, one thing will always be true about research: The process of finding things out means making connections. I clearly remember one night when I was walking up Essex Street in New York, near where I live. I saw a young couple fumbling with their iPhones and looking around at the street signs, trying to figure out where they were. (In case you were wondering, New Yorkers can spot lost tourists from two blocks away.) Finally, the young lady managed to look away from her smartphone long enough to ask me, "Excuse me, which way is Rivington Street?" I pointed them in the right direction, and they went happily on their way.

> **Research tools are merely ways for you to find out what someone else already knows.**

The tools you need to find out information are exactly that: They are means to serving a larger end. It doesn't matter whether you're busy Googling for a salient fact or working the phones to track down an expert at a federal agency; research tools are merely ways for you to find out what someone else already knows. They are remarkable, no doubt, and I am amazed each day at the power we have to locate the most exotic bits of information. But as you tackle projects, keep in mind one of the famous passages from E. M. Forster's novel *Howard's End*. "Only connect. . . . Only connect the prose and the passion and both will be exalted." Connect to websites, to books, and to your own imagination. But ultimately the secret to knowing how to find

> **Ultimately the secret to knowing how to find out anything means learning how to connect with people.**

out anything means learning how to connect with people. Exactly how you do it is up to you. Throughout this book, I've shown any number of ways to go about it, but in the end, you must ask the right questions, find the right resources, and, most important, connect.

ACKNOWLEDGMENTS

Every book is a walk across a tightrope in public. The blame for all its flaws may be laid at my door, but whatever strengths it may enjoy come from the work of many people whose encouragement and efforts have helped bring this book into print.

To my pals at Mediabistro.com, especially the indefatigable Taffy Brodesser-Akner, who gave this book its name, and the ever-supportive Carmen Sheidel, Laurel Touby, and the staff of the education programs.

To all the many students who attended the lectures that were the basis for this book, who patiently listened for three hours at a stretch on Monday evenings in rooms hot in July or cold in December, most often after trudging up four flights of stairs to a SoHo loft.

To my agent, Jim Levine; Kerry Spark; and the staff at the Levine Greenberg Literary Agency.

To my editors, Maria Gagliano and Christina Lundy at Perigee Books, as well as to copyeditor extraordinaire Lisa Kearns, whose hard work protected the reader from my editorial lapses in judgment.

To all of my law firm colleagues whose collective expertise in the art of finding information remains a proud model that should be shared with the world.

To Drs. Alan Cohen, John Golfinos, Jeffrey Wisoff, Neal Lewin, Valerie Peck and Alan Dolber.

And to the nameless librarian in the North Bellmore Public Library who once showed a seven-year-old how to find and sign out a book correctly.

I give all of you my thanks and gratitude.

Don MacLeod
New York, NY

INDEX

ABOUT THE AUTHOR

Don MacLeod has been a legal researcher for more than twenty-five years at a number of major law firms in New York City, where he has researched companies, people, and legal issues, and answered thousands of reference questions. Don is the author of two editions of the *Internet Guide for the Legal Researcher* and since 1995 has served as the editor of the monthly Thomson Reuters newsletter "Internet Law Researcher" and the government resources review *Internet Connection*. He is a member of the American Association of Law Libraries and the Law Librarians of Greater New York, and frequently lectures on research techniques for law librarians and lawyers. He was the creator and instructor for mediabistro.com's popular class "How to Find Out Anything," a three-hour research seminar designed for reporters, writers, and mid- to senior-level editors.